The Encyclopedia of
Collectibles

TIME
LIFE ®
BOOKS

Other Publications:
Library of Health
The Epic of Flight
The Good Cook
The Seafarers
The Great Cities
World War II
Home Repair and Improvement
The World's Wild Places
The Time-Life Library of Boating
Human Behavior
The Art of Sewing
The Old West
The Emergence of Man
The American Wilderness
The Time-Life Encyclopedia of Gardening
Life Library of Photography
This Fabulous Century
Foods of the World
Time-Life Library of America
Time-Life Library of Art
Great Ages of Man
Life Science Library
The Life History of the United States
Time Reading Program
Life Nature Library
Life World Library
Family Library:
    How Things Work in Your Home
    The Time-Life Book of the Family Car
    The Time-Life Family Legal Guide
    The Time-Life Book of Family Finance

The Encyclopedia of
Collectibles
Silhouettes to Swords

TIME-LIFE BOOKS, ALEXANDRIA, VIRGINIA

Time-Life Books Inc.
is a wholly owned subsidiary of
TIME INCORPORATED

Founder: Henry R. Luce 1898-1967

Editor-in-Chief: Henry Anatole Grunwald
President: J. Richard Munro
Chairman of the Board: Ralph P. Davidson
Executive Vice President: Clifford J. Grum
Chairman, Executive Committee: James R. Shepley
Editorial Director: Ralph Graves
Vice Chairman: Arthur Temple

TIME-LIFE BOOKS INC.
Managing Editor: Jerry Korn
Executive Editor: David Maness
Assistant Managing Editors: Dale M. Brown
(planning), George Constable, Thomas H. Flaherty
Jr. (acting), Martin Mann, John Paul Porter
Art Director: Tom Suzuki
Chief of Research: David L. Harrison
Director of Photography: Robert G. Mason
Assistant Art Director: Arnold C. Holeywell
Assistant Chief of Research: Carolyn L. Sackett
Assistant Director of Photography: Dolores A. Littles

Chairman: Joan D. Manley
President: John D. McSweeney
Executive Vice Presidents: Carl G. Jaeger,
John Steven Maxwell, David J. Walsh
Vice Presidents: George Artandi (comptroller);
Stephen L. Bair (legal counsel); Peter G. Barnes;
Nicholas Benton (public relations); John L.
Canova; Beatrice T. Dobie (personnel); Carol
Flaumenhaft (consumer affairs); James L. Mercer
(Europe/South Pacific); Herbert Sorkin
(production); Paul R. Stewart (marketing)

The Encyclopedia of Collectibles
Chief Researcher: Katie Hooper McGregor
Art Assistant: Mikio Togashi
Editorial Assistant: Dawn Patnode

Editorial Production
Production Editor: Douglas B. Graham
Operations Manager: Gennaro C. Esposito,
Gordon E. Buck (assistant)
Assistant Production Editor: Feliciano Madrid
Quality Control: Robert L. Young (director),
James J. Cox (assistant), Daniel J. McSweeney,
Michael G. Wight (associates)
Art Coordinator: Anne B. Landry
Copy Staff: Susan B. Galloway (chief),
Diane Ullius Jarrett, Cynthia Kleinfeld,
Brian Miller, Celia Beattie
Traffic: Jeanne Potter
Correspondents: Elisabeth Kraemer (Bonn); Margot
Hapgood, Dorothy Bacon, Lesley Coleman
(London); Susan Jonas, Lucy T. Voulgaris (New
York); Maria Vincenza Aloisi, Josephine du Brusle
(Paris); Ann Natanson (Rome). Valuable assistance
was also provided by: Judy Aspinall, Karin B.
Pearce (London); Carolyn T. Chubet, Miriam
Hsia, Christina Lieberman (New York); Mimi
Murphy (Rome).

The Encyclopedia of Collectibles
was created under the supervision
of Time-Life Books by
TREE COMMUNICATIONS, INC.
President: Rodney Friedman
Publisher: Bruce Michel
Vice President: Ronald Gross
Secretary: Paul Levin

The Encyclopedia of Collectibles
Editor: Andrea DiNoto
Art Director: Sara Burris
Text Editor: Colin Leinster
Director of Research: Heidi Sanford
Research Coordinator: Cathy Cashion
Photographers: David Arky, Steven Mays
Assistant Art Director: Christopher Jones
Art Assistant: David Nehila
Researchers: Victoria Balfour, Carole Anne Fabian,
Jaclyn Fierman, Deborah Gale, Carol Gaskin,
Amy Gateff, Jannika Hurwitt, Nancy Jacobsen,
Jay Stevens, Russell Stockman, Susan Wasserstein,
Anne Yarowsky
Writers: Judson Mead, Ellen Posner,
David Schraffenberger, Jozefa Stuart,
Henry Wiencek
Editorial Assistant: Kathleen Hushion

Editorial Consultant: Jay Gold
Consultants for this volume: Monroe Fabian
(Silhouettes); Al Young (Silk Pictures); Edmund
Hogan, Sophia Snyder (Silver); Jane Brennan
(Smoking Paraphernalia); Anton Hardt (Spoons);
Gary and Diana Stradling (Staffordshire); John W.
Salomon, Ira Zweifach (Stamps); Gary Kirsner,
Jack Lowenstein (Steins); Ellen Paul Denker, Susan
Myers, Gary and Diana Stradling (Stoneware);
Leonard Garigliano, Andrew Mobrey (Swords)

For information about any Time-Life book, please write:
Reader Information
Time-Life Books
541 North Fairbanks Court
Chicago, Illinois 60611

Library of Congress Cataloguing in Publication Data
Main entry under title:
  The encyclopedia of collectibles.
  Includes bibliographies.
  1. Americana. 2. Antiques—United States.
I. Time-Life Books.
NK805.E63   745.1'09'0973   77-99201
ISBN 0-8094-2764-8
ISBN 0-8094-2763-X lib. bdg.

The Cover: Collecting souvenir spoons has been an
American avocation since the 1890s. Most of the
14 pictured on the cover are mementos of
American cities, although one *(fourth from top, left)*
commemorates George DuMaurier's novel *Trilby*,
and several are from foreign countries. The
souvenir of Salem, Massachusetts, decorated with a
witch *(third from bottom)* is particularly desirable.

Acknowledgments: silhouettes, top, page 18, Rosemarie
Lewis; silhouettes, page 19, Wania Jean Reynolds;
postcards, top, page 25, John High; silk pictures, pages 26-
29, Al Young; tureen, pages 30-31, The Metropolitan
Museum of Art, bequest of Jacob Ruppert, 1939; teapot,
page 32, The Metropolitan Museum of Art, bequest of A.
T. Clearwater, 1933; Paul Storr hallmark, page 34, by
courtesy of the Worshipful Company of Goldsmiths; all
other hallmarks, page 34, reproduced from *Bradbury's Book
of Hallmarks*; coffeepots, page 36, coffeepot, left, page 37,
all items, page 39, mustard pot, page 40, sauceboat and nut
dish, page 41, eggcup stand, page 42, wine taster and
goblet, page 45, pitcher and tray, page 47, sugar tongs,
center, ice tongs, bottom, page 52, flask, page 57, F.
Gorevic & Son, Inc.; platter, page 38, three handles, top,
page 51, James Robinson, Inc.; sardine box, page 40,
pepper grinder, page 43, wine labels, page 45, frames,
page 55, James II Galleries, Ltd.; napkin ring with bud
vase, page 43, International Silver company; place setting,
page 49, John R. McGrew; all items, page 50, asparagus
tongs, top, page 52, fish server, top, page 53, Wyler, Inc.;
humidor, page 60, tampers, top, page 67, all items, page
68, snuff box, top, page 69, brazier and tongs, page 70,
plug cutter, page 73, U.S. Tobacco Museum; roly-poly,
page 61, tin container, top left, page 63, Lester Barnett;
tobacco tin, page 62, Dolly and George Yanolko; top three
cigarette holders, cigarette cases, page 66, Rita Sacks,
Limited Additions; cigarette holder, fourth from top, page
66, Eva Jewelry & Antiques; table lighters, page 70,
Speakeasy Antiques; all items, page 88, all items, page 92,
Gary and Diana Stradling; all items, page 89, Gem
Antiques; marks, pages 90-91, adapted from *Encyclopedia of
British Pottery and Porcelain Marks*, edited by Geoffrey A.
Godden, © Geoffrey A. Godden FRSA, 1964, used by
permission of Crown Publishers, Inc.; pitcher, page 93, La
Ganke Antiques; Toby jugs, pages 94, 95, bust, page 96,
statue, left, page 97, Leo Kaplan Antiques; statue, right,
page 97, Ann Phillips Antiques; stamps, top, second row
left, third row center and right, bottom row center, page
98, stamps, pages 102-111, 116, three stamps, top, page
117, stamps, pages 118, 119, stamps, top row, middle row,
bottom left, page 120, stamps, page 123, Dumont Stamp
Co., Inc.; stamps, second row center and right, third row
left, page 98, Linda Slocum; stamp, page 99, cover, page
100, three stamps, top, page 101, William Sumits for *Life*;
stamp, center, page 101, Harmer Rooke & Co., Inc.;
covers, pages 114, 115, Patricia Siskin; stamps, bottom,
page 117, Ira Zweifach; mugs, page 128, Kermit Dietrich;
jug, page 142, The New-York Historical Society; drawing,
page 153, adapted from *The American Sword, Seventeen
Seventy-Five to Nineteen Forty-Five*, by Harold L. Peterson;
swords and guard, pages 156-157, Leighton R. Longhi;
saber, top, page 160, The Soldier Shop, Inc.; sword,
bottom left, page 160, Smithsonian Institution.

Contents

Silhouettes
Portraits from Paper and Scissors

Louis XV of France had a minister of finance, Étienne de Silhouette, who was such a renowned penny pincher that his name became a synonym for doing anything on the cheap. So, naturally, inexpensive paper cutouts of a person's profile became known as portraits *à la* Silhouette.

Silhouettes long ago outgrew the opprobrium of the finance minister's name to become popular as works of art and, more recently, as treasured collectibles. A daughter of King George III of England, Princess Elizabeth, was an amateur silhouettist—and so was the German philosopher-poet Goethe. In the 1770s the status of the silhouette was given a boost by the Swiss mystic Johann Kaspar Lavater, who proclaimed that an expert examination of a silhouette could reveal the character of the subject *(page 11)*.

The silhouette, in some cases painted but generally cut out of paper, was the snapshot of its day: an instant

Most silhouettes were cut from paper, but the one above was painted in black and highlighted in gold. It was made in the early 1800s; the ornate frame is a Victorian addition.

Dr. W. Lehman Guyton is a surgeon who shares his avocation with his wife. They started their collection of 300 silhouettes with the one that is shown on this page, a family heirloom.

memento, a lover's keepsake, a family picture. The artist snipped the profile of a subject in just a few minutes, most often using only paper and scissors; some dexterous practitioners could do it in seconds. Many ambitious artists were not content with an unadorned profile. They added depictions of clothing and hair in paint, or pasted a full-length silhouette onto a background to create a vignette that captured the character and social standing of the subject—and brought a higher fee.

Painted embellishments on a simple black-and-white profile can add value if they are well executed. In the example at left, the pink bonnet was painted in watercolor onto a silhouette, also painted, of an unknown lady of the early 1800s. Like most old silhouettes it is unsigned.

Two distinctive techniques arose, one of them more common in Europe, the other popular in America. In most European silhouettes, the profile was cut out of black paper and pasted onto a white background. Artists in America developed a method, called hollow-cut, that was the opposite: The profile was cut out of paper; what was left was then mounted on silk or paper of a contrasting color—ordinarily black but sometimes brown or red. The profile itself generally was discarded, although in some instances it might be saved or sold along with the hollow-cut piece.

So popular was the silhouette in the United States during the 18th and 19th Centuries that hundreds of professional artists set up silhouette "museums" or traveled from city to city to cater to the fashion. Some of them obtained machines that more or less automatically traced a profile *(page 11)*, to the amazement of the subject. Silhouette artists also did a brisk business selling profiles of such famous personages as Washington, Jefferson and Franklin, usually copied from engravings.

For silhouette collectors, the subject depicted influences value, but more important are age and the artist. Serious collectors concentrate on late-18th and early-19th Century works, although interest in 20th Century silhouettes has been increasing. A pre-Civil War profile is much more desirable than a late-Victorian one, and any example from 18th Century America is extraordinarily valuable. There are several ways to tell age if there is no trustworthy provenance: The name of the subject or the artist may be written on the silhouette, clothing styles indicate period, and ink color in writing may be a clue—the old inks eventually turned brown.

Identification information adds to value, particularly if it is written on the silhouette itself or on a label on the back. The best identifications are, first, the artist, and second, the subject. Date and place are also desirable.

Full-length silhouettes are more sought after than

A jovial old man in a high hat was profiled around 1800 by Charles Willson Peale, a noted Philadelphia portrait painter who had a machine to help patrons draw their own silhouettes.

busts, and group silhouettes, such as portraits of a family, are prized still more. A hand-cut silhouette of any date is more desirable than a machine-drawn silhouette of the same time unless the latter is a vintage example by a known profilist who finished the work by hand. To detect machine drawing, look for impressions left in the paper by the machine stylus.

If the artist is a famous professional such as Auguste Edouart, William Henry Brown or Martha Anne Honeywell, collectibility increases accordingly. Much less valued are the works of legions of anonymous itinerants who roamed through New England and the South.

The profilist who is considered by collectors to have been the most accomplished and whose work is most highly valued today was Edouart. A Frenchman who went to England and then to America in 1839, Edouart toured America's cities and spas, including the famous Saratoga Springs in New York, where he cut silhouettes of the wealthy and celebrated. He made thousands of likenesses of leading citizens, including Presidents John Quincy Adams and John Tyler, Senators Daniel Webster and Henry Clay, and General Winfield Scott.

William Henry Brown, another itinerant profilist who flourished in the 1830s and 1840s, was renowned for his ability to cut a silhouette of a person he had seen for just a few minutes. It was his practice, on arrival in a new town, to ask someone to point out the mayor and other leading citizens on the streets. He then cut their profiles and used them as advertising to lure other clients.

Brown did not limit himself to simple portraits; he won fame for a six-foot nine-inch silhouette of the *DeWitt Clinton*, an early railroad train, and a gigantic 25-foot silhouette of the St. Louis fire department, including a fire engine, two hose carriages and 65 firemen. He sketched these subjects on the scene; then at home he made a clean rendering and used it as a guide to cut out a silhouette on sections of paper that were inconspicuously joined into a continuous strip.

Two silhouette prodigies of the 19th Century whose works are much sought were Martha Anne Honeywell and Sanders Nellis. Both were born without hands. Miss Honeywell, as she was billed in her advertisements, managed to cut silhouettes by holding the paper in her toes and working the scissors with her mouth. Sanders Nellis made silhouettes by working the scissors with his toes—he then filled out his act by playing the cello and shooting an arrow into a quarter at 10 yards.

One name to watch for on silhouettes is Jean Millette. Although Millette has been credited with no fewer than 24,000 profiles of early Americans, including Washington, Jefferson, Hamilton, John Adams and John Paul Jones, he never existed. The profiles signed with that name are all late-19th Century fakes *(right)*.

Millette is the best-documented completely fictitious silhouette artist, but there are a great many other fake silhouettes—modern pictures bearing the forged names of actual artists. In the 1920s, when collecting old silhouettes first became widely popular, thousands of antique silhouettes were forged. Many are signed, falsely, with the name of the noted artist Charles Willson Peale (a true example of his work is pictured at left). In the early 1800s Peale had set up a silhouette museum in Independence Hall in Philadelphia. There he and an assistant, a black man named Moses Williams, cut profiles and embossed them with a stamp that read "Peale's Museum," "Museum" or simply "Peale." The stamp was easily forged and in the 1920s it was added to hundreds of silhouettes to increase their value.

A collector who is offered a Peale can look for signs that may indicate fakery—although no single bit of evidence is conclusive. For example, an embossed seal such as Peale used is easily forged and it should not be trusted as proof of origin. The edges of the cut paper are another clue; many fakes have ragged edges, especially around the mouth and nose, because forgers are rarely as careful as the original artist was. And consider the subject as well as technique. It is wise to be wary of portraits of famous people—particularly if a number of copies seem to be available. Famous names are favorite frauds because they fetch high prices.

The widespread use of photography from the 1840s onward eventually made the silhouette obsolete as a medium of portraiture, but the art remains very much alive. In city department stores and resort amusement areas and at fairs and craft expositions, artists continue to snip silhouettes for a few dollars. Though a modern practitioner has yet to make a reputation in the manner of William Henry Brown by snipping a 25-foot Saturn rocket, silhouette artists will be fashioning portraits for as long as people cast shadows.

Supposedly a Revolution-era silhouette of Alexander Hamilton, this profile by "Jean Millette" is a fake—the epaulet, high collar, and wide sleeves and lapel were fashionable later.

The Artist Who Never Was

The silhouette reproduced above is one of the huge number that once were ascribed to Jean Millette, a nonexistent artist. Jean Millette silhouettes first appeared in 1892 at an exhibition in New York City. They were not exposed as frauds until the 1970s—long after they had fooled many experts. Millette portraits of Washington and Jefferson were given to President Franklin D. Roosevelt with considerable fanfare in 1933, and in 1955 The Metropolitan Museum of Art in New York acquired several. The forger has never been identified.

Faked silhouettes are amazingly common. Some forgeries can be detected by comparing their style with that of genuine specimens. And many fakers give themselves away, as Jean Millette did in his Hamilton picture, by including anachronistic clothing details.

A note on the frame identifies Captain Jonas Satterlee and his wife Eliza, who sat for their profiles at Scudders Spectaculum in New York on their wedding day in 1826.

Although Susan A. Tagart is not a noted historical figure, the inscription of her name and birth date adds value to the silhouette above.

The delicately detailed hair and gauze collar were drawn in ink on a cut silhouette of Nancy Bradburg (above), whose name is on the back.

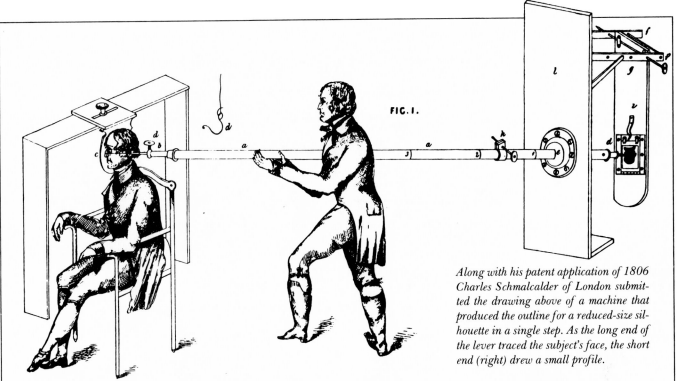

FIG. I.

Along with his patent application of 1806 Charles Schmalcalder of London submitted the drawing above of a machine that produced the outline for a reduced-size silhouette in a single step. As the long end of the lever traced the subject's face, the short end (right) drew a small profile.

Machines to Make Profiles

The making of silhouettes did not escape the march of mechanization in 18th Century Europe. A Swiss "scientist" named Johann Kaspar Lavater claimed that accurate silhouettes, if properly interpreted, could reveal personality. For his studies Lavater invented the prototype of the candle-and-chair apparatus shown at left, which made it possible to trace a person's shadow precisely. This large tracing was then reduced in size with the aid of a pantograph—a draftsman's device that is used to make a larger or smaller copy of an original.

The silhouette machine above carried Lavater's mechanization a step further; the operator would guide the talon of a machine over the contours of the subject's face while the machine simultaneously reduced the outline in size. Most silhouettes drawn by machine were not as graceful as handmade portraits, and they are accordingly less valuable today.

In this 18th Century engraving of a machine invented by Johann Kaspar Lavater, a shadow is cast on parchment. An artist traces the outline, which later would be reduced.

The decorations around this silhouette are characteristic of Pennsylvania Dutch folk art. The heart at the bottom suggests that the profile, mounted on silk, might have been done for the lady's sweetheart. Her name, and that of the artist, are not known.

Portraits of a family in Hartland, Vermont, were cut around 1820. Collars were shaped from the remaining paper, and other clothing was painted on. The fact that this is a group to which some painting has been added makes it a desirable collectible.

For two MISS days only
HONEYWELL'S
Splendid Gallery of
CUTTINGS
AND
Needle Work,

IS NOW OPEN AT Mr Williams's Hotel

THOSE Persons therefore, who wish to obtain their family likenesses, (cut in a few seconds, by Miss Honeywell;) are invited to embrace the present opportunity.

This interesting Lady, though born

WITHOUT ARMS,

Has acquired such use of a common pair of Scissors, by holding them in her *Mouth*, as to be able to cut out of paper, the most curious and difficult pieces of

CUTTING,

Ever attempted, such as the likenesses of distinguished

Americans and Europeans:

Together with a variety of others, such as Watch Papers, Flowers, Landscapes, and even the Lord's Prayer, perfectly legible; not only the outlines, but to resemble copperplate engravings. She writes, draws, and does all kinds of Needle Work, with the utmost facility and ease. She has travelled through Europe, where her work has been universally admired. An extensive variety of specimens of her elegant performance, are for exhibition in the house she occupies. All her elegant works are for sale. She can be seen at her various occupations, from 10 o'clock, A. M. till 9 P. M.

Admittance, including a Profile Likeness, (cut in a few seconds, without hands, by Miss Honeywell,) 25 cents; Children half price.   [*Printed at the Office of the Columbus Sentinel.*

The simple silhouette of Isabella Ann Bishop at right is the work of an extraordinary woman, Martha Anne Honeywell, who was born without arms. She held the paper in her toes and cut it with scissors held in her mouth, as she noted on her work and boasted in the handbill above, which advertises one of her regular appearances in East Coast cities. Silhouettes made by her are valuable.

Cut by M. Honeywell with the mouth

Isabella Ann Bishop
Taken in 1826

Among the most sought-after silhouettes are full-figure profiles on a lithographed background. This one was made in Newport, Rhode Island, by Samuel Metford, an Englishman who worked in the United States.

William Henry Brown, one of the best-known 19th Century silhouette artists, cut this full-length portrait of Elizabeth Remington around 1840. Brown's work is prized for its great detail, displayed here in the careful cutting of the flowers and bows, the use of white highlights, and the shadow on the floor — a subtle touch.

Auguste Edouart, considered by many connoisseurs to be the best of all silhouette artists, depicted the entire McCurdy family (right) while they were vacationing at the fashionable spa of Saratoga Springs, New York, in 1844. The documentation, the number of figures and the identity of the artist combine to make this silhouette uniquely desirable.

T. F. Mc. Curdy.
Saratoga 16th Aug.t 1844.

Sarah L. Mc.Curdy.

Miss G.M.Mc.Curdy

F. Ward cut the two portraits above in the 1930s at Atlantic City. His stamp appears on both silhouettes—documentation that makes them *valuable. Atlantic City in the 1920s and 1930s, like Saratoga Springs in the 19th Century, was a favorite haunt of silhouette artists.*

Novelties in Silhouette

Silhouettes by 20th Century artists— many of whom designed commercial novelties or cut profiles in department stores or resort concessions— first attracted collectors in the 1970s. They are easily found in attics, at rummage sales or at flea markets— some of the most interesting silhouettes decorate such stationery-store items as wall hangings, greeting cards and place cards *(left)*.

Celluloid silhouettes (left) for place cards show figures from Flossie Fisher's Funnies, a magazine series of 1910 to 1918.

An artist at the John A. Brown department store in Oklahoma City cut these portraits of the McGinnis family in 1934. The little girl at right, who became Mrs. Wania Jean Reynolds, found them a few years ago when her mother (center) was clearing a trunk of family mementos. The name of the artist is not known, but his skill with detail, such as the girl's glasses and bow, could make a collection of his work valuable.

MUSEUMS
Essex Institute
Salem, Massachusetts 01970

Massachusetts Historical Society
Boston, Massachusetts 02215

National Portrait Gallery
Washington, D.C. 20560

BOOKS
Carrick, Alice Van Leer, *A History of American Silhouettes, 1790-1840.* Charles E. Tuttle Company Inc., 1968.

Oliver, Andrew, *Auguste Edouart's Silhouettes of Eminent Americans, 1839-1844.* University of Virginia Press and National Portrait Gallery, 1978.

W. F. Cody = Buffalo Bill

WOVEN IN PURE SILK BY T. STEVENS, COVENTRY. ENG.

BUFFALO BILL.

(COL. W. F. CODY.)

P.T.O.

Silk Pictures
Tiny but Detailed Tapestries

There is a small footnote to the destructive bombing of Coventry, England, in World War II that is important to silk-picture collectors. On the afternoon before the city was leveled in 1940, the production manager of the Stevengraph Works happened to take home with him a volume containing samples of all the woven silk pictures and illustrated bookmarks produced by the company since its beginning in 1862. In the morning the factory was completely gone. So were the houses on either side of the manager's, but the volume of samples in his house was safe. The only com-

Lewis Smith is a New York City lighting consultant who acquired 167 of the 188 known silk pictures called Stevengraphs.

plete collection of the world's most sought-after silk pictures, it is now in the Coventry city museum.

Silk pictures are machine-made scenes that were a popular novelty in the late-Victorian era. Generally 2½ by six or seven inches and crammed with minute detail, they were mounted on cardboard and displayed on a wall, like tiny tapestries. Similar illustrations were woven into bookmarks, political ribbons, souvenirs and postcards. The mechanism that made this possible was the Jacquard attachment, with which the operation of a loom could be programed on punch cards to make practically any desired design. (For a description of the Jacquard device, see the article on Coverlets in a separate volume of this encyclopedia.) Preparing a set of cards for a complex design was a painstaking process—one picture could take as many as 5,000 cards—but once programing was done, a loom could make identical pictures endlessly and speedily. Automation allowed manufacturers to sell the pictures for a few cents apiece.

Illustrated ribbons, bookmarks and souvenirs were first produced in large quantities in the 1860s. They were made in several European countries and America. But Thomas Stevens' Stevengraphs, so popular they form a class by themselves, did not appear until 1879.

Thomas Stevens issued this woven silk portrait of William F. Cody— Pony Express rider, buffalo hunter and showman—in 1887. That was four years after Cody first brought his Wild West show to Europe. This Stevengraph, popular with English and American collectors, is rare.

In that year the first Stevengraph *(page 24)* was woven and mounted on cardboard as part of an exhibit at a fair in York, England. Over the next three decades, Stevengraphs depicting 188 different themes were produced. Around World War I, silk pictures went out of style, but the works in Coventry continued producing a few Stevengraphs until the time of World War II.

The range of Stevens' subjects was broad. Portraits of English and German royalty were made along with depictions of politicians, boxers and jockeys. Coaches, trains and battleships were favorites, as were hunting, tennis and cricket scenes. Historical subjects included Lady Godiva's ride and the death of Nelson. Some of the rarest have brought more than $1,000 each, but most can be found for a tenth of that.

The rarity and condition of a Stevengraph determine its value—and the cardboard mount is important. At a London auction in the late 1960s a copy of *The Present Time (page 22)* with a broken mount brought only a tenth as much as the same picture with a mount intact. *The Meet* in a remounted version brought a quarter of the price fetched by the same picture in the original mount.

Information on the back of the mount can help the collector determine the date of a Stevengraph. On labels affixed to the backs, Stevens placed the titles of other Stevengraphs that were available. Since he registered the designs, the most recent date among the titles listed indicates the approximate date of the picture.

Besides rarity, the quality of the color influences value. The dyed silk in woven illustrations is affected by exposure to sunlight; faded examples are less valuable. At auction a sunstruck copy of *The First Point* brought only a sixth as much as the same picture with good color. Pictures produced in the late 19th Century are generally more valuable than those of the early 20th because their colors are more subtle and the scenes more detailed.

The silk pictures most avidly sought by American collectors are the relatively few Stevengraphs with pictures relating to the United States. These include depictions of such notables as Buffalo Bill, President and Mrs. Grover Cleveland, boxer John L. Sullivan, George Washington and Sergeant G. H. Bates, a Union soldier who carried the American flag throughout the South after the Civil War. Other prized American subjects are Niagara

STEVENGRAPH PURE SILK WOVEN PICTURES.

TEN HIGHEST PRIZE MEDALS & DIPLOMAS
AWARDED TO THOMAS STEVENS.

REGISTERED

STEVENGRAPH WORKS,
COVENTRY.

AND AT
114, NEWGATE ST.
LONDON.

REGISTERED

MARK

MARK

The following subjects can be had beautifully Illuminated in 10 or 12 colours:

THE GOOD OLD DAYS (Royal Mail Coach) | THE START (A Race Scene)
THE PRESENT TIME (Railway Train) | THE STRUGGLE (Companion to above)
TURPIN'S RIDE to YORK (The Toll-gate Leap) | THE LAST LAP (A Bicycle Racing Scene)
FULL CRY (A Hunting Scene) |

THOMAS STEVENS, Sole Inventor and Manufacturer,
STEVENGRAPH WORKS, COVENTRY.

The label at the left lists not only the picture below but six other Stevengraphs then available—information that, when compared with registration dates, fixes the time of issue of this picture. Of the titles listed, The Start *was the last to be registered, on December 15, 1879. On later issues of* The Present Time, *this label was replaced by an eight-title label, including a title registered on December 22, 1879. So this example of* The Present Time *was probably mounted for sale during the week between December 15 and 22 of that year.*

The locomotive Lord Howe *pulls two coaches in an early Stevengraph. First issued as Stephenson's 'Triumph'—in honor of George Stephenson, inventor of the steam railroad—it appeared in several versions, including a very rare one that showed part of a third coach.*

WOVEN IN SILK BY THOMAS STEVENS, INVENTOR AND MANUFACTURER, COVENTRY AND LONDON. (REGISTERED)

The Present Time.
60 MILES AN HOUR.

Falls, the signing of the Declaration of Independence *(below)* and a baseball game.

Some of the great rarities among Stevengraphs are pictures that have errors. One famous example is a British fox-hunting scene, *The Death,* on some copies of which a loom attendant absent-mindedly used blue thread for the hunters' coats instead of the traditional red. Other rarities were created by the happy-go-lucky freedom that Stevens and his workers allowed themselves in printing titles and the company name on the front of the pictures. They changed typefaces for different issues of the same picture. They used the same title for different pictures. They altered the credit line—two different inscriptions were used on the earliest Stevengraphs. One reads "Manufactured in York Exhibition, 1879," the other "Woven in the York Exhibition, 1879." Both are rare, but the first is the rarer of the two.

The great popularity of Stevengraphs overshadows that of silk pictures from American and French manufacturers, and these other works are much less valuable. This is true even though French pictures *(page 27)* are rarer than Stevengraphs and are considered esthetically superior—they have finer detail and take many of their subjects from paintings. American pictures also are bargains, although so many have world's fair or political themes that collectors in those fields are buying them up. The most collectible American silks are those that show American scenes.

Stevengraphs are so widely known that bargains are now difficult to find except at an estate sale at which you happen to be the only knowledgeable buyer. Many pictures are sold through mail auctions, advertised in collectors' periodicals. American silks are often sold at shows for collectors of political and world's fair memorabilia. Examples may turn up in flea markets in the region stretching west into Pennsylvania from Paterson, New Jersey, the city established by Alexander Hamilton in 1792 as a model textile-manufacturing center.

Unmounted Stevengraphs can turn up even in a junk shop. A fellow collector once came into such a shop in time to see a young fellow purchase four unmounted Stevengraphs for a few cents apiece. He was going to patch his bluejeans with them.

For related material, see the articles on Embroidery, Handbags, Quilts and Samplers in separate volumes of this encyclopedia.

A Stevengraph of John Trumball's famous painting is a rarity much sought after by American collectors, but the breaks that can be seen in the mount of this example sharply decrease its value. The same painting also appears on the back of the two-dollar bill introduced in 1976.

A detail (left) of the first silk picture issued by Thomas Stevens (below) reveals the remarkable intricacy of the weaving. This picture, originally called The 'London & York' Stage Coach, commemorates the first running, in 1706, of that important mail route. Like other Stevengraphs, this one has been issued with a variety of backgrounds.

WOVEN IN SILK BY THOMAS STEVENS, INVENTOR AND MANUFACTURER, COVENTRY AND LONDON. (REGISTERED)

The Good Old Days.

Silk postcards and greeting cards like these were a Stevens specialty. This version of the ride of Lady Godiva through Stevens' native Coventry is common; another version, without the peeping Tom in the window, is rare. The flag card was sold aboard the liner Arabic.

This woven silk picture of the Tower of London—made for the Stevengraph firm's 1931 calendar—is valuable because few survive and because it is in excellent condition. The same picture was sold without the calendar as a mounted Stevengraph and is extremely rare in that form.

LITTLE BO-PEEP

LITTLE BO-PEEP
HAS LOST HER SHEEP,
AND CAN'T TELL
WHERE TO FIND THEM;

LEAVE THEM ALONE,
AND THEY'LL COME HOME,
WAGGING THEIR
TAILS BEHIND THEM.

LITTLE JACK HORNER

LITTLE JACK HORNER
SAT IN A CORNER,
EATING A
CHRISTMAS PIE;

HE PUT IN HIS THUMB,
AND PULL'D OUT A PLUM,
AND SAID,
"WHAT A GOOD BOY AM I!"

I LOVE LITTLE PUSSY

I LOVE LITTLE PUSSY,
HER COAT IS SO WARM,
AND IF I DON'T HURT HER,
SHE'LL DO ME NO HARM.

I'LL SIT BY THE FIRE
AND GIVE HER SOME FOOD
AND PUSSY WILL LOVE ME,
BECAUSE I AM GOOD.

TO MY PET

DOLLY, YOU'RE
A NAUGHTY GIRL,
ALL YOUR HAIR
IS OUT OF CURL,
AND YOU'VE TORN
YOUR LITTLE SHOE.
OH! WHAT MUST
I DO WITH YOU?
YOU SHALL ONLY
HAVE DRY BREAD,
DOLLY, YOU SHALL
GO TO BED.

DO YOU HEAR,
MISS, WHAT I SAY?
ARE YOU GOING
TO OBEY?
THAT'S WHAT MOTHER
SAYS TO ME,
SO I KNOW IT'S
RIGHT, YOU SEE;
FOR SOMETIMES
I'M NAUGHTY, TOO,
DOLLY, DEAR, AS
WELL AS YOU.

Children's bookmarks with Victorian nursery rhymes were issued by Stevens in 1874. Not as valuable as Stevengraphs, they have the same high quality of detail because they were made on the same machinery. Many bear the same illustrations and texts.

JACQUARD

A French silk picture in black and white (above) was produced by Neyret Frères, as were the others on this page. It honors the inventor of the device that wove silk pictures.

This French silk picture is based on The Swing, a painting by the 19th Century painter Pierre Auguste Cot, who also painted the original of the picture at right.

The detail and shading visible in The Storm (above) are strong points of French silk pictures. Though rare, this example is not as valuable as a Stevengraph of comparable rarity.

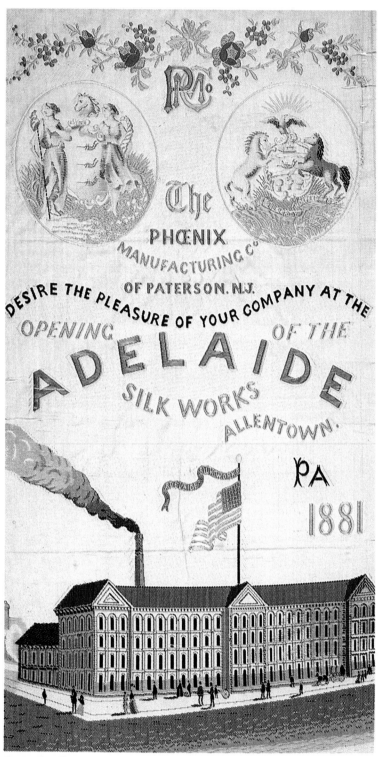

Woven in silk in Paterson, New Jersey, an invitation to the opening of a branch plant promotes the company's work. American giveaways in silk are rare.

A silk souvenir of the World's Columbian Exposition in Chicago in 1893 is desirable because of its detail, self-documentation, and American scenes and symbols.

A silk-picture souvenir of the St. Louis Exposition shows the Liberal Arts Building in the background and the exposition's fountains in the fore- *ground. It was produced by the National Silk Manufacturing Company of Paterson, which was demonstrating its looms at the fair.*

MUSEUMS AND LIBRARIES
Huntington Library, Art Gallery and Botanical Gardens
San Marino, California 91100

The Passaic County Historical Society
Lambert's Castle
Paterson, New Jersey 07503

Paterson Museum
Paterson, New Jersey 07501

Smithsonian Institution
National Museum of History and Technology
Washington, D.C. 20560

COLLECTORS ORGANIZATIONS
Stevengraph Collectors' Association
Daisy Lane

Irvington-on-Hudson, New York 10533

BOOKS
Baker, Wilma Sinclair LeVan, *Silk Pictures of Thomas Stevens.* Exposition Press, 1957.

Bunt, Cyril G. E., *The Silks of Lyons.* The Dolphin Press, 1960.

Godden, Geoffrey A., *Stevengraphs.* Associated University Presses, Inc., 1971.

Nelson, William, and Charles A. Shriner, *History of Paterson and Its Environs.* Lewis Historical Publishing Company, 1920.

Sprake, Austin, and Michael Darby, *Stevengraphs.* Chaucer Press, 1968.

Silver
Useful Luxuries to Treasure

When Admiral George Dewey was to be honored in 1899, his admirers sought a gift that not only would be appropriate for him as the Hero of Manila but also would be indicative of America's newly won eminence in the world. So 70,000 dimes, roughly 90 per cent silver in content, were solicited from the people of the United States, melted down and cast into a huge loving cup blanketed with nationalistic emblems and gleaming with the shine of this noble metal. Gold could have been chosen as a more valuable material, of course, but gold coins were

Dorothy Thornton Rainwater, who has written six books on silver, specializes in silver objects from the Victorian period.

not plentiful in the pockets of average people, while nearly everybody had some silver, a metal precious enough to perform the lofty function.

This episode reveals the duality of silver objects of all kinds. For millennia they have served as symbols of high status, proudly handed down from generation to generation. Yet even families of modest means own some pieces, including many that, although not solid silver, are valued for their beauty and history.

Much inherited silver lies neglected in attics and basements because it went out of style. In the late 1960s a New York man who happened on a silver bowl in his attic parted with it and some napkin rings for $12. Almost immediately that bowl was resold for $7,500. It proved so valuable because it was solid silver, very old and the work of a noted silversmith of the period in a style popular among modern collectors—characteristics that can be recognized if you are familiar with the basics of silver collecting.

Though some collectors specialize in works of a particular design or a certain maker, most concentrate on one of three main collecting categories—tableware such

This mighty 1807 soup tureen and tray is the work of Paul Storr, one of the most famous of the gifted silversmiths active in Georgian London. In 1979 a table service—dinner plates and matching serving dishes—by Storr brought more than half a million dollars.

31

Paul Revere is the most esteemed of all American silversmiths and his work is the most valuable to collectors. Revere made this solid-silver teapot in his Boston shop in 1796 in the neoclassical style known as Federal. Other silversmiths of the time produced pieces that are comparable in craftsmanship, but Revere's are the most desirable because of his fame as a patriot of the American Revolution.

as teapots and trays; the forks, spoons and other dining implements classified as flatware; and personal items such as hatpins and picture frames. (Jewelry is described in a separate volume of this encyclopedia.) Some of the most sought-after pieces were made in America, but fine work from England and other European countries was imported in quantity and it too is prized by American collectors.

Objects dating to the 17th Century are exceptionally rare, and the oldest silver generally collected is from the 18th and early 19th Centuries. However, the great outpouring of silverware that began in Victorian times and has continued since provides huge quantities of handsome and interesting pieces that are not difficult to find.

Most of the very old objects and the most valuable of the more recent ones are solid silver. But solid silver comes in various grades. The commonest formulation in Great Britain and the United States since the mid-19th Century has been sterling, in which 925 parts out of 1,000 are silver, the rest being copper. This is the quality of an object bearing an English hallmark *(box, page 34)*. On 19th Century American solid silver you may find the word "coin" (C), "dollar" (D), "standard," "premium" or "sterling," none of which signified an official standard of purity, but generally indicated silver about 90 per cent pure. These terms also provide a rough dating guide. "Coin" first came into use around 1830, "sterling" around 1860. After 1906, American silver marked "sterling" indicated the same purity as British sterling.

Plated silver is of two types. The more valuable is Sheffield plate, a heavy body of copper fused to a top layer of silver (and sometimes also a bottom one). Most Sheffield, manufactured only from its invention in 1742 until it was superseded by electrical plating in the 1840s, is not marked. Pieces stamped "Sheffield," "Real Sheffield" or "Genuine Sheffield" are later, electroplated imitations—less valuable but still desirable. Sheffield can be recognized by examining the edge, where the copper body is generally concealed by a soldered covering of silver *(page 38)*.

In producing both solid silver and Sheffield, the silvery material is formed first and then shaped into a piece of silverware. Not so with electroplated silver. It is shaped first of a base metal, then coated with a thin veneer of silver. Distinguishing electroplate from solid silver is difficult. On heavily worn plate the base metal may show; otherwise a chemical test is necessary.

The prestige of the silversmith adds value to both solid silver and silver plate. Among the outstanding 18th and early-19th Century smiths—all of whom worked only in solid silver—are Paul Storr of London, the Revolutionary hero Paul Revere, Samuel Kirk of Baltimore and one of the very few women to achieve fame in this field, Hester Bateman, of a family of noted London silversmiths. Several of the later American firms that are especially noteworthy—Tiffany & Co., Gorham Mfg. Company, Reed & Barton and the Meriden Britannia Company—produced fine silver plate as well as solid silver. Among the outstanding specialists in plate were James W. Tufts and The Pairpoint Corporation.

Solid silver from England is clearly marked to identify maker and date of manufacture *(page 34)*, but identifying other wares may be more difficult, requiring a knowledge of styles and pattern details. Silver styles progress from the early neoclassical through the revivals of the 19th Century—Egyptian, Greek, Oriental, rococo, Renaissance—to Art Nouveau, a style avidly collected now, and the more recently popular Art Deco. All these styles have enjoyed recurrent periods of popularity, and many continue to be reproduced today. Thus, telling a truly old piece from a newly produced example may hinge on distinctions in patina or details of pattern.

As important to value as the quality of metal, the maker and the workmanship is condition. Worn silver plate can be replated—a process that improves resale value— but it is a mistake to try replating pieces with heavily pitted surfaces because the design can seldom be salvaged. Tarnish generally can be removed, but deep scratches and corrosion are serious flaws. Some owners and dealers remove monograms from pieces by buffing—a destructive step that is unnecessary because a monogram seldom detracts from value.

Most of these considerations apply equally to solid silver and plate. One concern, however, mainly affects collectors of solid silver: burglary. The price of silver metal has increased so much—by more than 500 per cent in less than one year—that collections of solid silver are often stolen, sometimes to be resold as art objects and sometimes simply to be melted down for their metal. I keep my valuable items in bank vaults, and all collectors must pay careful attention to insurance and locks.

In one sense worse than the burglars are those misguided people who melt down sterling silver that has passed out of style. When Mrs. Grover Cleveland arrived in Washington in 1886 as the just-married bride of the 22nd President-elect of the United States, she was welcomed by many Americans as a figure of grace and youthful beauty in the presidential mansion. But because she ordered the silver commissioned by Dolley Madison some 75 years earlier to be melted down and recast in a more modern style, Frances Cleveland left a name forever tarnished in the minds of silver collectors.

LANGUAGE OF THE SILVERSMITH

This glossary defines the more important terms used by silversmiths and silver collectors to describe metal standards and various techniques of decoration.

BEADING: Ornamentation, as along a border, with a continuous row of tiny hemispheres.

BRIGHT-CUT ENGRAVING: Engraving in which metal is removed by beveled cutting tools to form reflective facets.

CHASING: An incised, fine design created by hammering the outer surfaces using small, sharp tools that do not cut away any metal.

COIN: An alloy composed usually of 900 parts per 1,000 of silver.

DIE: A metal stamp used to create an ornamental design.

ELECTROPLATING: Electrical method of coating a base metal with a thin layer of silver.

FINE SILVER: Metal that is 999 parts pure silver per 1,000, essentially pure silver.

FLUTING: Parallel concave vertical panels. The term is also loosely used to refer to convex ornamentation of this sort, which is more properly called reeding.

GADROONING: Ornamentation, usually on a border, with parallel raised ovals resembling twisted rope.

MATTING: Deliberate dulling of a surface with fine punches or scratches.

PIERCING: Ornamental perforations resembling lace.

PLATE: In British usage, solid silver of sterling standard or higher, not to be confused with plated silver in British usage or silver plate in American.

PLATED SILVER: In British usage, electroplate.

RAISING: The process of hollowing a flat sheet of metal by alternately hammering and heating it.

REEDING: Narrow vertical convex panels.

REPOUSSÉ: High-relief ornamentation produced by hammering from the back or from the inside.

SHEFFIELD PLATE: Thin sheets of silver and copper fused together.

SILVER PLATE: In United States usage, electroplate.

STERLING: An alloy of 925 parts fine silver per 1,000, standard in England since the 1300s.

THREADED: Bordered with fine raised lines.

THE VENERABLE HALLMARKS OF BRITISH STERLING

Identifying British sterling is simple because an explicit marking system was established in London in the 1300s and has continued in use in various forms ever since. Any piece that is made of sterling—92.5 per cent pure silver—is stamped with hallmarks, proof that the silver meets all requirements of the silversmiths' guild, or hall, hence the name. By the latter part of the 18th Century, silversmiths in London were using five marks, illustrated in the photograph below of a plate made in 1810 by Paul Storr. The first mark on the Storr plate identifies it as his with his initials—initials always serve as a maker's mark. The second, or standard, mark authenticates the material as English sterling. The third, or town, mark indicates that the material was assayed—tested for purity—in London. The fourth is a code that identifies the year in which the object was produced, and the fifth mark attests

to the payment of duty during the reign of King George III.

Reproduced in the columns underneath the Storr hallmark are some symbols for standard, town and duty marks (the last were required only between 1784 and 1890). Each of the assay towns developed its own particular dating code, but the most important is the one for London, part of which is illustrated in the second column from the right.

In 1478 London began marking each year's work with a different letter of the alphabet. A 20-letter sequence was used: A through U, with the J omitted. (In 1975 the sequence was expanded to 25 letters.) The type style of the letter and the shape of the shield encompassing it were changed at the beginning of each 20-year series; the examples on this page show the letter P as it appeared in six succeeding alphabets.

HALLMARK STAMPS ON A PAUL STORR PLATE OF 1810

| MAKER'S MARK | STANDARD MARK | TOWN MARK | DATE LETTER | DUTY MARK |

STERLING STANDARD MARKS	TOWN MARKS	LONDON DATE-LETTER STYLES	DUTY MARKS
ENGLAND UNTIL 1821	LONDON UNTIL 1821	1796-1815	GEORGE III 1784-1820
ENGLAND SINCE 1821	LONDON SINCE 1821	1816-1835	GEORGE IV 1820-1830
SCOTLAND	SHEFFIELD	1836-1855	WILLIAM IV 1830-1837
IRELAND	BIRMINGHAM	1856-1875	VICTORIA 1837-1890
	EDINBURGH	1876-1895	
	DUBLIN	1896-1915	

Popular among collectors are 19th Century tea sets like the five pieces above, made by Gorham of sterling silver with the high-relief decoration that is called repoussé. The set consists of a sugar bowl, at center, and (clockwise from bottom left) a waste, or slop, bowl (for cold tea), an eight-inch-high coffeepot, a teapot and a creamer. The design indicates that the tea service was made in the 1890s.

Tableware

The Victorians had an insatiable passion for novelty, and they indulged it heartily in buying silver tableware and accessories. The formal table of a century ago shone with mechanical servers: Butter dishes had tops that rolled open; condiment holders called casters operated like Ferris wheels to offer a choice among Worcestershire, hot sauce and piccalilli; ice-water pitcher sets were supported by frames for easy pouring. Even pieces that were not mechanical contrivances were elaborate in other ways. Compotes, saltcellars, toothpick holders and servers designed for specific foods from sardines to nuts were lavishly ornamented, many with little figures of cupids, cherubs and animals such as squirrels and porcupines.

These novelties—the more outlandish the better— have become popular tableware collectibles. Uncountable numbers of them were produced, and because most are plated rather than solid silver, they are generally less costly to buy than older, solid wares.

Tableware includes much more than Victorian novelties, of course, and many collectors seek old pieces resembling those still made today: trays, bowls, platters and particularly tea sets, in either solid or plated silver. The most desirable are handmade objects of the 18th and early 19th Centuries in the simple Federal and Empire styles, but these have become very rare. When factory production of silver began in the 1840s, the wares first copied the patterns of earlier silversmiths. These styles, as well as all the later ones, can be seen in the tea sets, solid silver and silver plate, that are particularly popular among collectors. Tea sets, which were initially a luxury of the very rich, had become almost a staple of the middle-class American home by the late 19th Century, and many sets have survived. Small sets comprising three or four pieces are quite easy to find. Of the highest value are matching sets of seven or more pieces, including separate pots for coffee, tea and hot water (sometimes marked respectively 7, 6 and 5, which indicates the

This French coffeepot, made around 1800, is prized for its side handle, three legs and pear shape, but all French tableware of that period is rare—most was melted to pay for wars.

The style of the 1880s Viennese coffeepot at right was fairly common on the European continent at the time, and it is less valuable than the French pot shown above.

capacity in half pints), and a sugar bowl, creamer, waste bowl and tray.

Some dealers put together sets of pieces that closely resemble each other, and such an assembled set is naturally worth less than one originally manufactured as a unified group. One way to check the authenticity of a set is to look for a maker's catalogue number on the bottom of each piece. Some manufacturers put the same number on each piece, often four digits, but sometimes two or three. These catalogue numbers should not be mistaken for dates.

Tea sets have been prized by collectors for some two

centuries, but a newer item of tableware that has enjoyed a surge of popularity is the silver-plated napkin ring with a sculpted figure. Particularly desirable are the rings that are decorated with characters from the children's stories of Kate Greenaway, an English writer and watercolorist who was well known in England and America from the 1870s onward. Kate Greenaway figures have been widely reproduced, so the collector should carefully examine all the details—in particular the fingers—of the figure, which are sharp in the originals and indistinct in copies.

Veteran collectors sometimes buy pieces that have

The lion finial on the lid and the mask below the spout of this English pot are typical of the cast decorations that are popular among silver-plate collectors. The style suggests the pot was made between 1860 and 1880.

The American firm of Reed & Barton, highly regarded by collectors, displayed this silver-plated coffeepot at the 1876 Philadelphia Centennial. The angular handle and high legs were common designs during the 1870s.

been broken or are in disrepair; replating may increase the value of plated pieces, but restoration reduces the value of solid wares and those with glass sections. Such items as mustard pots, casters, and bride's baskets for flowers or fruit are valuable only if the piece still has the original glass in good condition. A silver-plated dinner-caster frame without its glass cruets is practically worthless. Similarly, all the parts of an English-made sterling-silver object—the lid and body of a tankard, for example—should be examined to see that they have the same hallmarks. Because the smaller parts of many American-made sterling objects are unmarked, a collec-

tor must have a sharp eye to detect a replaced part.

On a silver-plated object the repair or replacement of a part is less objectionable—since it was machine-made to begin with—if the repair is well done. For example, a missing finial on a teapot can be replaced by a cast made from the matching finial of the coffeepot in the same set, and look fine. Repaired pieces often can be detected by the soldering outlines left after a missing handle, say, has been replaced. Here a little warm, moist air helps. Breathe on a piece suspected of having been soldered. Condensation often will show where soldering has been done—in sterling as well as silver plate.

This meat platter was made in England around 1810 of desirable Sheffield plate, the fused silver-copper sandwich that preceded electroplated silverware. Most Sheffield is unmarked but can be recognized by its edges. An enlargement of the underside of the tray (below) shows the border of silver that was soldered onto the edge to hide the copper layer, thus forming a lip that can be felt.

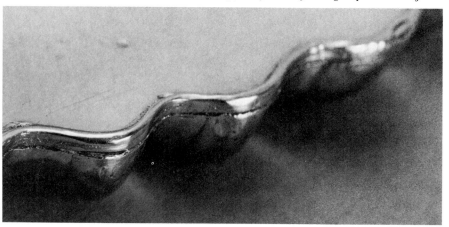

The handle on the cover of this English silver-plated vegetable dish can be removed (inset) so that the cover can be turned over and used as a second serving dish. These large serving dishes are fairly common in silver plate but hard to find in sterling.

No silver maker's products are more highly prized than those stamped with the name of Tiffany & Co. Its Chrysanthemum pattern, seen in the two-handled sterling tray above, is especially prized by collectors. This piece was made between 1891 and 1902.

An Austrian silversmith fashioned this mustard pot of solid silver in the 1880s. Its original glass liner is missing, a lack that reduces the value by at least a fourth.

The container above is a 19th Century English biscuit box, a popular Victorian piece that is fairly easy to find.

Sardines were a favorite treat in the 19th Century, and a covered silver-plated dish (above), known as a sardine box, was made to hold the aromatic delicacy. Many of them have tiny fish finials on their lids.

The coin-silver sauceboat at left is a rare piece from the 1830s, made by a New York silversmith, Marquand & Company.

Nut dishes are relatively common, in both plate and sterling, but they are popular with collectors. This example, hand-wrought of sterling around 1900 in Baltimore, depicts a country scene in the repoussé work that the city's silversmiths were famous for.

Silver-plated cake baskets like the one below are widely available. The medallions date this one to the 1860s. It was made by Meriden Britannia Company of Meriden, Connecticut, whose products are favored by many collectors.

Eggcup stands—egg casters—are popular among collectors, especially if, like this plated example, they are complete, including the tray, spoon holder and the usual complement of six cups.

Napkin rings are among the most sought after of silver-plated items. Even sterling rings, if plain, are not nearly as valuable as decorated silver-plated rings such as this one combined with a vase.

Sterling pepper grinders such as this 1902 London example are quite rare and valuable, although plated mills are fairly easy to find.

Saltcellars are much more common than pepper grinders. This 1860s Gorham dish is decorated with then-popular Classical medallions.

This silver-plated spoon warmer—a container of hot water—heated a spoon to prevent chilling of the porridge. The nautilus design was the most common shape of this avidly sought collectible.

The Meriden Britannia Company patented this unusual wine-bottle holder in 1881. It surrounded the bottle, opening and closing on hinges, and was fitted with a felt lining to cushion the bottle and keep the contents at serving temperature. Such holders were popular accessories for picnics during the 19th Century. They now are difficult to find but are not highly valued by collectors.

The shallow dish at left is a silver-plated wine taster made in France or Great Britain. Many similar ones were imported to the United States and are now common. They are not marked as silver plate and should not be confused with more valuable 18th Century solid-silver tasters; almost all the solid-silver ones are marked.

The coin-silver wine goblet above was made by the Ball, Tompkins & Black Company of New York City, whose products are prized.

Silver-plated labels (left) for wine and liquor bottles are widely available. Collectors specialize in one of the many different shapes and patterns popular in the 1800s. Some labels were plain rectangles, but others had decorations of flowers, or the grape motif shown here.

This 1824 water pitcher, fashioned in coin silver by Samuel Kirk of Baltimore, is the collector's prize. Its marks and Empire ornamentation, unique to Baltimore silver of this period, revealed to the collector that the pitcher was worth more than its price tag of $125.

The solid-silver water pitcher and tray above are in the Art Nouveau Martelé series that was produced by Gorham from 1895 to 1910.

Pieces of this series were handmade and are among the most desirable of American-made Art Nouveau silver.

Flatware

There is such an amazing variety of silver flatware that many collectors specialize in one type or one pattern. Flatware includes not only knives, forks and spoons but also serving pieces—a number of them far from flat, such as ladles, scoops and tongs.

Matching sets of flatware were uncommon in the United States before the 19th Century—until then even the rich made do with a limited, if costly, assortment of utensils. But Victorian fashion decreed elaborately formalized table manners, which initially sought to prevent crude eating with the fingers and eventually set up complex rules assigning a special tool and technique to every imaginable foodstuff. Hostesses looked to manuals of etiquette for instruction. A work portentously titled *Decorum: A Practical Treatise on Etiquette* allowed some individual choice at table but generally laid down the law: "Pudding may be eaten with the fork or the spoon. . . . Never bite fruit." There was a certain amount of controversy in the area of cheese. *Decorum* insisted, "Cheese *must* be eaten with a fork." But *Etiquette for Americans* was equally clear: "Never . . . take cheese in your fingers. Eat it with a knife."

By about 1860 an American place setting might consist of 15 pieces: five forks, four spoons, four knives, and a spoon and a fork just for dessert. As the century progressed, so did the complexity of dinner- and flat-ware. By 1880 Reed & Barton offered 42 different shapes of knives, forks and spoons, with matching serving pieces for every purpose.

From this engaging diversity collectors may choose to concentrate on one kind of implement, a period, a style, a maker or even one maker's special pattern. Spoons, for example, have attracted collectors for some time. Some look for early-19th Century spoons, now very valuable, made in America of coin silver. In the late 18th and early 19th Centuries, there were spoonmakers in virtually every American city, and there is intense interest among collectors in finding local work. The origin of a piece can influence its value; a Philadelphia collector, for example, will pay more for a spoon or fork made in that city than for one made in New Haven.

Serving pieces from the 18th Century also have their collectors. In the case of sugar tongs—a favorite with many collectors—the form of the piece can date it and thus establish its value as an antique. The earliest sugar tongs—from the early 18th Century—worked like scissors, with two pieces joined by a pin. In the second half of the 18th Century the familiar, and more readily found, U-shaped design came into use.

American-made place settings usually did not include dinner knives with matching handles until the middle of the 1860s. Before this time knife handles were usually

Nine tableware patterns that are popular among collectors—many of whom specialize in spoons—are depicted below with the names given them by the manufacturer and the dates during which they were in production. All of them are silver plate with the desirable trademark "1847 Rogers Bros." Of this group, the patterns that are most sought after are Assyrian Head and Charter Oak.

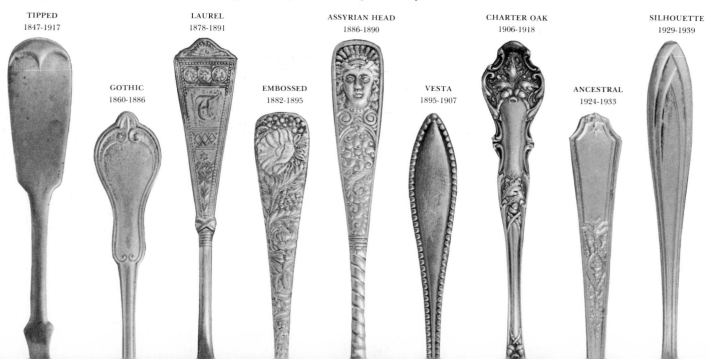

TIPPED 1847-1917		LAUREL 1878-1891		ASSYRIAN HEAD 1886-1890		CHARTER OAK 1906-1918		SILHOUETTE 1929-1939
	GOTHIC 1860-1886		EMBOSSED 1882-1895		VESTA 1895-1907		ANCESTRAL 1924-1933	

Most collectors of silver-plated flatware specialize in a pattern, and the design above is among the most popular, one of at least 62 other grape patterns known. This one, called Vintage and bearing the "1847 Rogers Bros." trademark, was introduced in 1904 and discontinued in 1918. The great popularity of the set led the makers to increase the number of pieces from the initial 65 to 101.

made of bone or ivory, and the blades were made of steel—not by a silversmith but by a cutler.

Patterns, which are fairly easy to recognize, also provide a means of dating because, once factory production began, the patterns were listed in the manufacturers' catalogues. However, patterns continued in production over long periods, and some of the very old ones have been revived. The patterns bear names that collectors are familiar with today. Flatware that was designed to evoke European styles was called Venetian or Fontainebleu, for example, and floral styles were given names such as Orchid and Orange Blossom.

Among the patterns in flatware sought by many collectors of late-19th and early-20th Century sterling are Reed & Barton's Love Disarmed and Gorham's Versailles. Similar patterns are also available in less valuable silver plate. Among the makers whose products are sought are those of Rogers Bros., Meriden Britannia

Company and their successor, International Silver Company. Some of the most popular and valuable patterns in both solid silver and silver plate are those depicting grapes. Many collectors loosely refer to all grape designs as Vintage, but there is only one real electroplated Vintage pattern—the one that was produced by the International Silver Company and bears the "1847 Rogers Bros." trademark *(page 49)*.

Patterns trademarked "1847 Rogers Bros." are favored by many collectors of silver plate. But not everything marked "Rogers" is 1847 Rogers Bros. Many Rogerses unconnected with the original brothers—who made the first quality plated ware—sought to capitalize on the clout of the name. They joined silver firms that could then include the prestigious name in their trademarks. Before the Rogers of Rogers & Hamilton of Waterford, Connecticut, became associated with that silver manufacturer, he was a cigar dealer.

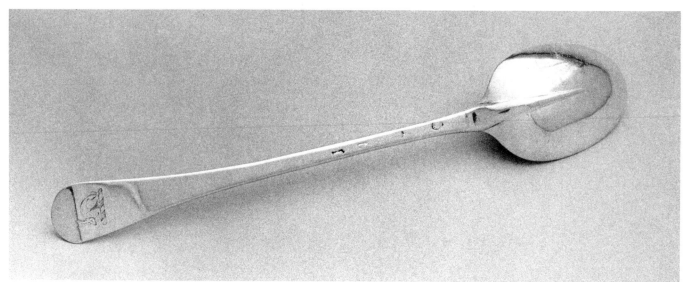

The long-handled sterling-silver basting spoon above was made in England in 1702 with a tapered ridge of silver (known as a rattail) under the bowl, a common decorative feature of 18th Century flatware. A family crest—a rabbit—is on the back of the handle.

Obsolete flatware forms such as the 1739 English marrow scoop above, used to get the tasty marrow out of beef bones, are a specialty of many collectors.

The 13-inch meat skewer above has hallmarks clearly visible on the left that identify it as English, made in London in 1799 by a silversmith named Wallis. It was used only for serving; while the meat was roasting, a wooden skewer acted as a stand-in.

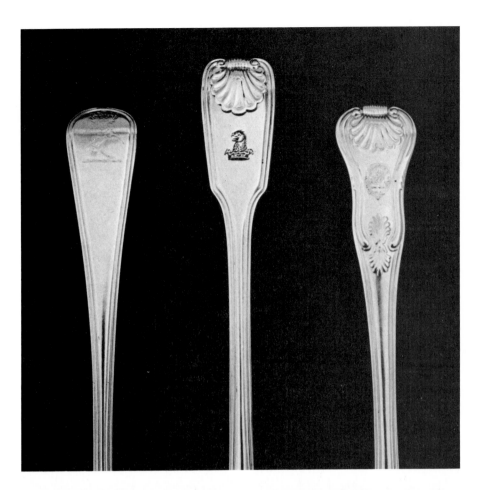

At right are three flatware patterns that collectors consider to be classics of the late 18th and early 19th Centuries. The design on the left is known as Thread and is the oldest and rarest. The center pattern added a shell to the older pattern and is called Shell and Thread. (The engraved figure below the shell is an owner's crest, not part of the pattern.) The most commonly found pattern is Kings, at right.

The 18th and early-19th Century coin-silver spoons shown above have handle designs known as (left to right) Old English, Coffin Handle, Basket of Flowers, Fiddleback and Tipped. The ladle-shaped spoon in the center is for mustard, the rest are for tea. The Tipped spoon shown was produced by J. Moulton of Newburyport, Massachusetts, whose family made silver articles for two centuries.

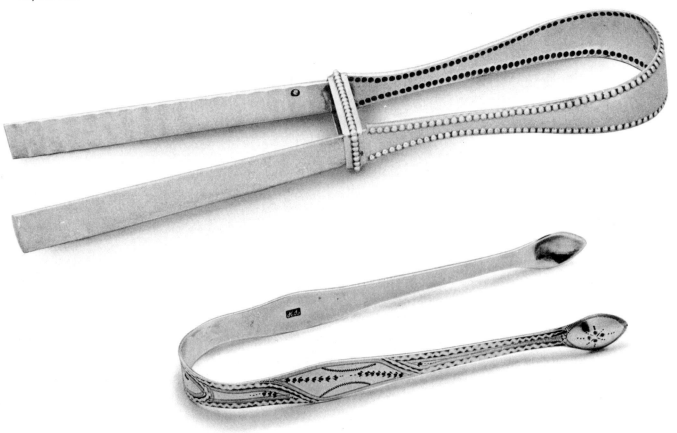

Tongs, made in a variety of shapes, are widely available. The silver asparagus tongs at top were manufactured in Amsterdam in 1860. The sterling sugar tongs above, dating from around 1785, bear the initials of the famous English silversmith Hester Bateman; anything with her mark brings roughly three times more than the work of most of her contemporaries. The coin-silver ice tongs below were produced in the middle of the 19th Century by William Gale & Son of New York City.

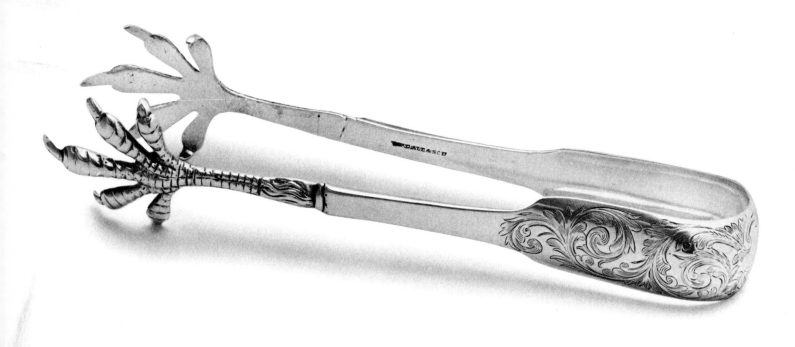

The three pieces on this page, known as slices, trowels, servers or spades, are examples of a popular collecting specialty. The 18th Century sterling server at right could have been used for fish or cake. Servers of this period and quality are very rare. The coin-silver American fish slice below has a pattern, designed by Michael Gibney in 1844, that was the first protected by a United States patent. The silver-plated server in the Crown pattern at bottom, made by Rogers & Brother between 1876 and 1898, is the least valuable of the three.

Once part of a matching set that graced a lady's dressing table, this silver-plated mirror is valuable because it is in the Art Nouveau style, *fashionable in America from approximately 1895 to 1920 and popular among collectors since the late 1960s.*

Personal Accessories

Ladies and gentlemen of high fashion in the Victorian era heaped themselves, their desks, bathrooms and dressing tables, as well as their dinner tables, with silver bric-a-brac. A well-turned-out gentleman might take a silver flask or collapsible silver cup on his travels. His valise had a silver tag, his umbrella a silver band. The lady's dressing table was a Comstock Lode of silver combs, hand mirrors, perfume bottles and perhaps a silver glove stretcher *(page 56)*.

It is still possible to find such items fairly easily. Some collectors regularly check thrift shops, where trays of miscellaneous junk may contain small pieces of silver. Sterling is usually marked as such, but it may or may not bear a manufacturer's mark, which adds value. The manufacturers whose products are prized include, as might be expected, Tiffany, Reed & Barton, and Gorham, but some unexpected ones as well: Unger Brothers, Alvin Manufacturing Company, Sterling Company

of Providence and William B. Kerr & Co. Unger Brothers made an extensive line of Art Nouveau articles that are now avidly sought by collectors.

Particularly desirable are complete dressing-table sets. A basic set for ladies consisted of comb, hairbrush and hand mirror, but some designs had as many as 20 pieces, including comb, brush, mirror, hatbrush, cloth brush, velvet brush, puff box, hairpin box, pin tray, jewel box, powder and cream jars, and manicure tools.

Much toiletware with Art Nouveau or Art Deco patterns was silver plate. Much plate is unmarked, so collectors look for desirable forms rather than makers.

For related material, see the article in this volume on Spoons, and the articles on Boxes, Buttons, Candleholders, Canes, Combs, Corkscrews, Hatpins, Inkwells, Knives, Matchsafes, Medals, Needlework Tools, Pens and Pencils, and Pressed Glass in separate volumes of this encyclopedia.

Small silver-plated vases like the one at left were common accessories in the 19th Century.

Two English picture frames (above), of sterling silver, illustrate the change in styles that took place in a few years at the beginning of the century. The ornately embellished frame at right was made in 1895, the much simpler one in 1908. Both forms are desirable but easy to find.

The sterling glove stretcher above is a fairly rare example of a device that appeared in the 1880s and was popular until around World War I. A finger of a tight-fitting kid glove was pulled over the beak of the bird and the crown feather was pressed down, expanding the beak to stretch the wet leather after washing so that the glove could be pulled on.

The cut-glass powder jar (left) and cream jar, both from around the turn of the century, have similar sterling lids but were made by different silver companies.

A sterling perfume bottle (left)—an accessory popular among collectors—was made in 1892 by William B. Kerr & Co.; it can be dated by its fleur-de-lis trademark (not visible), used by the company that year only. The container on the right is a pomander, which held powdered scent.

Boxes for hairpins, included in many matching sets for dressing tables, are now hard to find. Hamilton & Biesinger of Philadelphia made this sterling example in the 1890s.

Sterling desk accessories from the early 1900s are easy to find. This matched set includes (clockwise from top left) magnifying glass, eraser holder, letter opener and bookmark.

The logical companion piece to the collapsible cup at left might be a pocket flask. The cut-glass and sterling flask above is an 1884 work by the well-known English firm of Asprey & Company.

This silver-plated collapsible cup was meant for the vest pocket of a 19th Century gentleman. Many like it were made in the 1880s and 1890s, and a variety of styles can be found today.

A ceremonial drink from a tricky wedding, or wager, cup (right) was traditional at German weddings. The skirt, when inverted, formed a large cup for the groom to drink from while the small cup at top, swinging on pivots, was filled for the bride. Custom required the groom to tip the skirt cup up, fill it, drink from it and set the device back down without spilling any of the bride's portion. This example was probably made in the 19th Century.

MUSEUMS

The Art Institute of Chicago
Chicago, Illinois 60603

The Bayou Bend Collection
Museum of Fine Arts
Houston, Texas 77019

The Cleveland Museum of Art
Cleveland, Ohio 44106

Colonial Williamsburg
Williamsburg, Virginia 23185

The Detroit Institute of Arts
Detroit, Michigan 48202

Greenfield Village and Henry Ford Museum
Dearborn, Michigan 48121

Henry Francis du Pont Winterthur Museum
Winterthur, Delaware 19735

Historic Deerfield, Inc.
Deerfield, Massachusetts 01342

Los Angeles County Museum of Art
Los Angeles, California 90036

The Metropolitan Museum of Art
New York, New York 10028

The Minneapolis Institute of Arts
Minneapolis, Minnesota 55404

Museum of Art, Rhode Island School of Design
Providence, Rhode Island 02903

Museum of the City of New York
New York, New York 10029

Museum of Fine Arts
Boston, Massachusetts 02115

The New-York Historical Society
New York, New York 10024

Philadelphia Museum of Art
Philadelphia, Pennsylvania 19101

Sterling and Francine Clark Art Institute
Williamstown, Massachusetts 01267

Wadsworth Atheneum
Hartford, Connecticut 06103

William Rockhill Nelson Gallery and Atkins
Museum of Fine Arts
Kansas City, Missouri 64111

Worcester Art Museum
Worcester, Massachusetts 01608

Yale University Art Gallery
New Haven, Connecticut 06520

PERIODICALS

The Magazine SILVER, Silver Publishing Company,
P.O. Box 22217, Milwaukie, Oregon 97222

BOOKS

Bradbury, Frederick, *History of Old Sheffield Plate.*
Northend Publishers, 1912.

Carpenter, Charles H., Jr., and Mary Grace, *Tiffany Silver.* Dodd, Mead & Company, 1978.

Faith, Dennis, *Three Centuries of French Domestic Silver.* Metropolitan Museum of Art, 1960.

Fales, Martha Gandy, *Early American Silver.* Excalibur Books, 1970.

Holland, Margaret, *The Phaidon Guide to Silver.* Phaidon Press, Ltd., 1978.

Hood, Graham, *American Silver: A History of Style, 1650-1900.* Praeger Publishers, Inc., 1971.

Hughes, Bernard and Therle, *Three Centuries of English Domestic Silver, 1500-1820.* Frederick A. Praeger, Inc., 1968.

Hughes, G. Bernard, *Small Antique Silverware.* Bramhall House, 1957.

Jackson, Charles J.:
English Goldsmiths & Their Marks. Macmillan and Company, 1921.
An Illustrated History of English Plate. Country Life Ltd. and B. T. Batsford, 1911.

Kovel, Ralph M. and Terry H., *A Directory of American Silver, Pewter and Silver Plate.* Crown Publishers, Inc., 1961.

McClinton, Katharine Morrison, *Collecting American 19th Century Silver.* Charles Scribner's Sons, 1968.

Rainwater, Dorothy T.:
Encyclopedia of American Silver Manufacturers. Everybodys Press, Inc., 1975.
Sterling Silver Holloware. Pyne Press, 1973.

Rainwater, Dorothy T. and H. Ivan, *American Silverplate.* Thomas Nelson Inc. and Everybodys Press, 1968.

Schwartz, Marvin D., *Collectors' Guide to Antique American Silver.* Doubleday & Company, Inc., 1975.

Turner, Noel D., *American Silver Flatware, 1837-1910.* A. S. Barnes and Co., Inc., 1972.

Ward, Barbara McLean and Gerald W. R., *Silver in American Life.* David R. Godine, Publisher, Inc., 1979.

Smoking Paraphernalia
Reminders of Tobacco Pleasures

A humidor for pipe tobacco, made of lead in the late 18th Century, is adorned with a pheasant handle and a hunting scene. A presser inside compacts the tobacco to keep it moist.

Sailing through the Bahamas on October 16, 1492, Columbus saw some Indians carrying "dry leaves which must be something much valued by them, since they offered me some at San Salvador as a gift." A few weeks later two of his crew saw Indians smoking cigars. The leaves were tobacco, unknown outside the Americas. Within a few decades, Spanish and Portuguese explorers had seen the entire roster of Indian tobacco habits: smoking, tobacco chewing and snuff taking. And the rest of the world proceeded to try them all.

Each habit has had its seasons of popularity, and each has acquired paraphernalia, all of it collectible—from commercial packages and tobacconists' equipment to bejeweled cigarette holders. Pipe smoking became popular in the late 1500s, and pipe tools such as tampers are the oldest smoking collectibles. (Pipes are discussed in another volume of this encyclopedia.) Snuff is not smoked, of course, but it inspired the production of beautiful boxes (*pages 68 and 69*) that now are the

---

W. C. "Tobacco Bill" Hatcher of North Carolina, who began assembling his collection of smoking paraphernalia in the 1950s, is a wholesale buyer in the leaf-tobacco business.

---

most valuable of all collectibles associated with tobacco. In the 1800s cigar and cigarette accessories appeared. (Cigar labels also make up a large collecting field, described in another volume of this encyclopedia.) By the third decade of the 1900s the cigarette had pushed other forms of tobacco into a corner of the market, and few items made since then, except lighters and other cigarette accessories, are of much interest to collectors.

Of all collectibles related to tobacco that is smoked rather than snuffed or chewed, containers for pipe tobacco are the most desirable. Advertising premiums and small tools and accessories can be collected for a few dol-

lars each, though special items are exceptionally valuable. The rarest cigarette card, which is also the rarest baseball card, sold in 1979 for more than $3,000. And tools or accessories made of precious metals, such as solid-silver cutters for trimming the ends of cigars, bring high prices, as do those of great age, such as pipe tampers from the 1700s.

Containers for pipe tobacco—the bulk of most collections—are of two types. The older, originating in the 1600s and still made, is the tobacco jar, a container for storing tobacco and keeping it moist. The other is the lithographed tin in which most tobacco for pipes or roll-your-own cigarettes was sold in the first half of the 20th Century.

Tobacco jars were produced in such large numbers that even old ones are only moderately valuable. Many are illustrated in relief on the side. One illustration repeated on many jars commemorates a legendary scene from the earliest days of smoking: Sir Walter Raleigh's servant, on first seeing his master smoking, thinks he is afire and douses him with a flagon of beer. Most old tobacco jars were made of lead, but others are brass (a Dutch specialty), silver, pewter, pottery or wood. All except the wooden ones are more valuable than lead jars, and those made before 1900 are of principal interest.

The lithographed tin containers of tobacco appeared about 1870, were produced in huge quantities in the early decades of the 20th Century and virtually disappeared from the market after World War II. Some were made in eight, even 10, colors. In the early 1960s they could be had for a few cents apiece, but within a little more than a decade came to be regarded as great rarities

---

A tobacco tin called a roly-poly (right) was one of a set meant to serve as containers—probably for cookies—after the tobacco was used up. The Tin Decorating Co. of Baltimore issued roly-polys in sets of three or six for four different tobacco brands. Complete sets are very valuable.

worth hundreds of dollars. The valuable examples are those with elaborate decoration. Some were designed for secondary use after the tobacco was gone; a few had a brand name on one side and a label such as "flour," "sugar" or "salt" on the other. Tins were also made in the form of lunch pails, and these are desirable.

Not all pipe tobacco required an individual container. Much tobacco was sold in plugs—pocket-sized cakes of pressed tobacco from which a chunk could be bitten off for a chew or slices shaved off for a pipe. Most plugs were not even wrapped. Instead, the brand was identified by a tag, a small piece of tin clipped to the plug. The little bits of tin are a sizable collecting specialty: I have around 4,000 different ones, and I am still looking.

Before long, plug users were offered gifts for the tags they saved and sent back to the manufacturer, creating another collectible, the premium. For 10 tags the ardent user of the Pinkerton Tobacco Co. Tiger Stripe or Buckshoe brand got 50 feet of Irish-linen fishing line, or for 8,750 tags a horse-drawn buggy with a leather top.

Premiums proved so popular that special types were created, the best known being cigarette cards, introduced in the 1880s. These sets of small cards, generally bearing pictures and factual data, treated almost every subject from world leaders to dogs. Pictures of pretty women graced sets otherwise devoted to serious information on fish and flowers. In one famous set, explaining the international naval distress signals, the card for "I'm on fire" shows the appropriate signal pennant over a discordantly cool beauty. Other cigarette premiums include little booklets on such subjects as lives of Presidents or world history, oval or rectangular pieces of cloth printed to look like Oriental rugs, printed strips of satin called silks *(page 64)*, and small leather squares with college insignia. Most premiums are easy to find and are not very valuable. However, some complete sets of cards bring surprisingly high prices when offered for sale.

Although you cannot build a collection with chance finds, they are a treat when they turn up. I once discovered a tobacco tag I had long wanted in the back of a desk drawer in an abandoned barn. But that was nothing compared with the luck of an acquaintance who specializes in tags. He bought some old trout flies that came with spools of fly-tying silk. The silk, he noticed one day to his delight, was wrapped around tobacco tags.

For related material, see the articles on Advertising Giveaways, Baseball Cards, Boxes, Cigar Bands and Labels, Matchsafes, Pipes, Royal Souvenirs, Tinware and Tramp Art in separate volumes of this encyclopedia.

A pocket-sized tin of pipe tobacco, manufactured by S. A. Ilsley & Co. of Brooklyn for a Louisville, Kentucky, company, is prized for its subtle coloring and the slogan "I need thee every day," which is visible under the smoker's face. It is rare and very desirable.

Made for clothiers, a valuable lithographed tin container dated 1876 (above) was sold filled with detachable shirt collars. When the collars were removed, the buyer had a tobacco holder with a pouch.

This one-pound sack of loose smoking tobacco is collectible primarily for its brightly lithographed label, but its value is increased because the sack is still filled with tobacco and sealed with the original revenue stamp.

A wooden box of plugs of tobacco, bearing the date 1920 on the bottom, is valuable because it is full of its original tobacco, but it would be desirable

even if empty. The red tags embedded in the individual plugs, visible at the right, are themselves collectible (page 64).

Meant to be pasted onto a wooden tobacco crate known as a caddy, this 1874 lithographed paper label, measuring 6 by 12 inches, was never used.

Decorated and shaped bits of tin —the lion above is ½ inch long—were stuck into plugs of tobacco to identify brands. Millions of such tags were made for perhaps 12,000 brands, and they are widely collected.

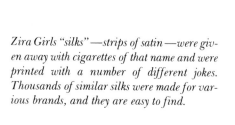

Zira Girls "silks"—strips of satin—were given away with cigarettes of that name and were printed with a number of different jokes. Thousands of similar silks were made for various brands, and they are easy to find.

The roll-your-own cigarette machine of the 1940s at right is complemented as a collectible by its original box and a package of tobacco. These devices are common.

The cigarette box at left contains its original cigarettes and card, increasing its value at least five times. The sliding cardboard box and name indicate an older, "Turkish" brand, replaced in popularity during the 1920s by blended brands in "cup" packages (right).

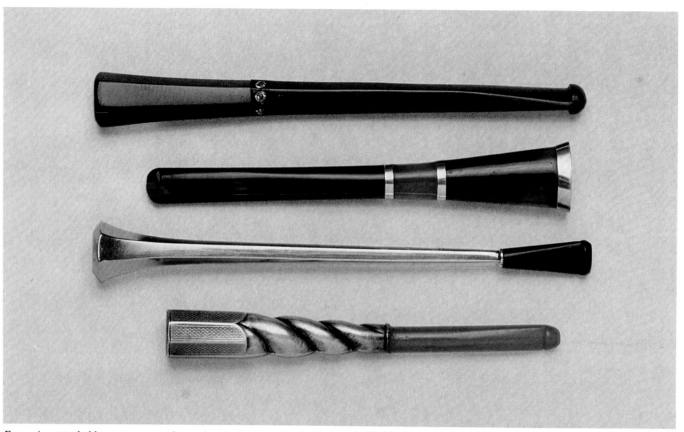

Four cigarette holders represent styles and materials popular in the 1920s and 1930s. They vary in desirability: The ladies' American plastic holder with rhinestones (top) is easy to find; the British tortoise-shell holder with gold bands is more valuable; the 14-karat gold stem of the holder second from the bottom makes it very valuable; the twisted silver-and-amber French holder at the bottom has moderate value.

A gold-plated cigarette case (left)—honoring the golden anniversary of Ignatz and Yettie Whitelaw—and an Art Deco enameled one are typical of those collectors seek. The inscription on the gold case adds value, as does the corner finger hole, which permits the end to be flipped open.

Pipe-bowl tampers from the late 1700s and early 1800s are valuable because of their age. The lady's leg is porcelain, made at the famous Meissen factory in Germany; the two fighters and the signet-ring tamper are both brass, produced in England.

Four cigar cutters of the turn of the century, including one (center) that apparently was a giveaway, are common American-made collectibles. The example at lower left has a bottle-cap lifter and is made of steel and silver, and hence is the most valuable. The others are steel.

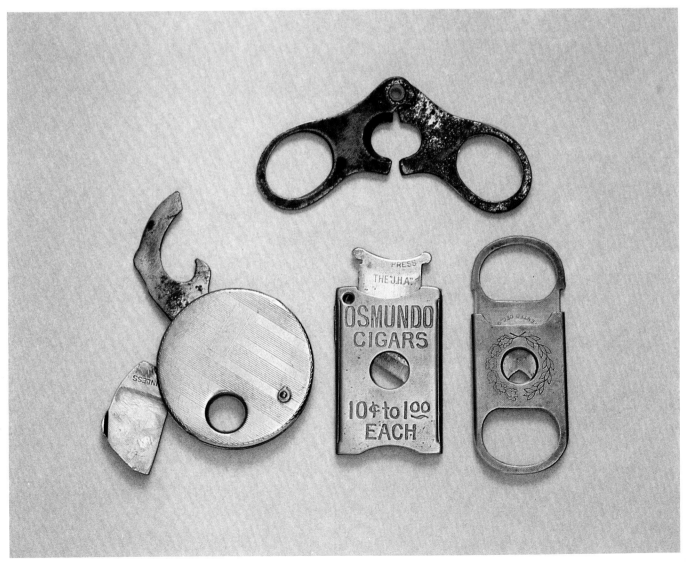

Small ivory snuff spoons from the late 1700s (above) had holes to filter out bits of tobacco too big to be sniffed comfortably.

A snuff container called a mull (right) is an old Scottish version of the snuff box. Made from rams' horns, many mulls had tools attached—this one includes the bones of a rabbit's foot to brush away spilled snuff, a pick, a spoon, a rake to level the mull's contents, and a hammer for knocking clumps loose.

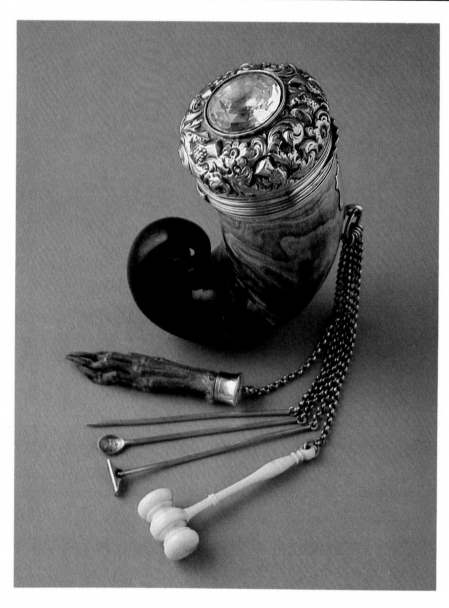

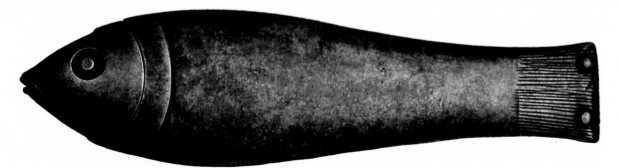

A six-inch-long tin snuff rasp is shaped like a fish. Its body lifts open at the gills to expose a flat, very fine grater to turn chunks of tobacco into powder. Snuff rasps disappeared in the 18th Century, when pre-ground snuff became available to tobacconists.

Fanciful Tools for Snuff

The accouterments of snuff taking are the most elegant of collectibles associated with tobacco, including not only elaborate and costly containers but also a variety of tools like those at left. It was said in the 1700s that breeding could be recognized by the ritualistic flourish with which a man—or a woman—tapped and opened the snuff container and offered it to others.

Snuff is powdered tobacco, to which such flavors as apple, eucalyptus, mint or orange may be added. Although in the United States today it sometimes is chewed, in centuries past it was sniffed into the nostrils, generally producing a tremendous sneeze.

The most important of the many accessories used for sniffing tobacco is the snuff container. While Dr. Samuel Johnson, the famous English writer and lexicographer, and Frederick the Great of Prussia carried their snuff loose in their pockets—Dr. Johnson had his pockets lined with leather—the less eccentric but well-to-do sniffer was more likely to use a small box *(top right)* or a bottle like the ones shown at bottom right.

The wealthiest are said to have had a different box for every day of the year. Gold and jewel-encrusted boxes were everyday baubles for royalty and aristocrats. Many snuff boxes were decorated with beautifully executed miniature paintings. When such boxes come onto the auction market, they can command tens of thousands of dollars; a snuff box that belonged to Catherine the Great of Russia was sold at auction for $150,000 in 1979.

Snuff bottles, which have been imported to the United States from China in large numbers since the 19th Century, are also valuable. They were fashioned not only of glass but also of jade, ivory, porcelain and many other materials; glass bottles, however, are the easiest to find.

An early-19th Century papier-mâché snuff box from Leipzig, then part of Saxony, depicts Napoleon, who had invaded the country, attempting to gobble the city.

Three Chinese snuff bottles of the 19th Century are (from left): agate with a stopper of Peking glass made to resemble stone, jade with a jade stopper, and glass with a Peking glass stopper.

The brass brazier at right and the tongs above were standard pipe smoker's implements before the advent of matches. The brazier held hot coals, one of which the smoker picked up with the tongs to light his pipe.

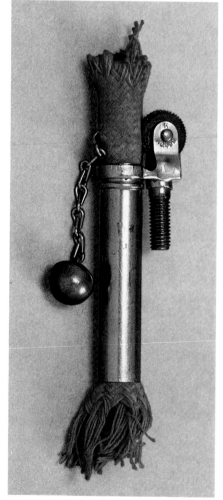

A simple rope lighter for troops in World War II was lit with flint and steel. It smoldered rather than flamed, thus showing no light when used in a trench at the front.

Table lighters like these from the 1930s and 1940s are easy to find, as are most of the thousands of different lighters made since World War I.

This eight-inch-high lighter, pictured with the cigarettes it advertised, stood on a tobacco counter. The wick is wrapped around a removable steel rod in the camel's hump. When the rod, grasped by the gold ball, was struck against a strip of flint near the forelegs, the wick flamed.

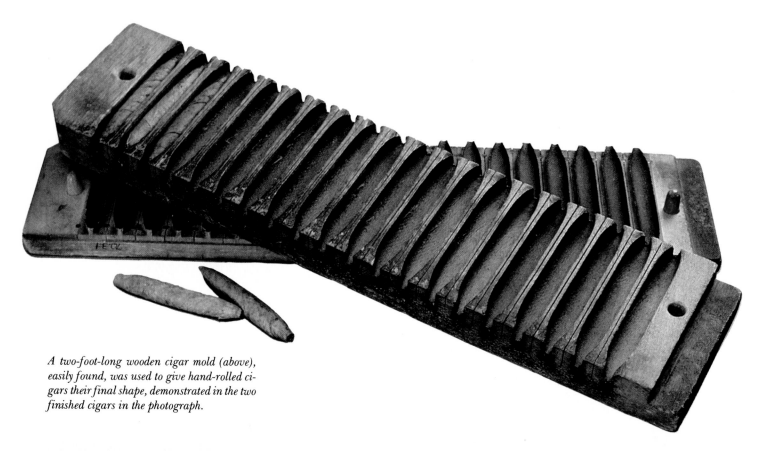

A two-foot-long wooden cigar mold (above), easily found, was used to give hand-rolled cigars their final shape, demonstrated in the two finished cigars in the photograph.

This cigar buncher was used to stack cigars; when the rack was full, the cigars were tied in a bundle with the ribbon, which in actual use would have been placed with the name facing down. Small cigarmaking shops were common well into the 20th Century, so bunchers are easily found.

An imp thumbing his nose sits atop the handle of a late-19th Century plug cutter, a device used in stores to slice tobacco into usable pieces. The handle operates a guillotine-like blade in the device. Cutters like this one, once common, are now moderately valuable.

MUSEUMS
U.S. Tobacco Museum
Greenwich, Connecticut 06830

Valentine Museum of Life and History
Richmond, Virginia 23219

COLLECTORS ORGANIZATIONS
Cigarette Pack Collector's Club
c/o Richard Elliott
5 Governors Avenue
Winchester, Massachusetts 01890

International Snuff Bottle Society
2601 North Charles Street
Baltimore, Maryland 21218

Tin Container Collector's Association
P.O. Box 4555
Denver, Colorado 80204

BOOKS
Blakemore, Kenneth, *Snuff Boxes.* Frederick Muller Ltd., 1976.

Pinto, Edward H., *Wooden Bygones of Smoking and Snuff Taking.* Hutchinson & Co. Ltd., 1961.

Robert, Joseph C., *Story of Tobacco in America.* Alfred A. Knopf, 1952.

Scott, Amoret and Christopher, *Tobacco and the Collector.* Max Parrish and Co., Ltd., 1966.

Spoons
A Special Kind of Gift

Among the old stories that have been told and retold about traveling salesmen, one happens to be true: From the 1890s until the 1920s, these drummers had a penchant for souvenir spoons. They bought thousands of them and took them home as mementos of towns in their sales territories. That passion for these souvenirs was shared by other Americans who traveled, and silver manufacturers produced a variety of designs.

Spoons commemorated scenic wonders, noteworthy events or famous people. Many spoons were decorated with Christmas themes; among the most desirable with a

Barbara Prince frequently sets up displays of her collection of souvenir spoons in libraries and schools.

religious theme are Apostle spoons, sets of 13 bearing figures of Christ and the Twelve Apostles. Some spoons were created for specific cities (typically showing a new building). Others were stock designs adapted for local use. A picture of a stagecoach being robbed appeared on the handles of spoons shipped to many cities in the West, for example; there was space in the bowls for local jewelers to add such inscriptions as "La Junta Colo" and "Livingston Mont." Some illustrations were naturalistic—local wildlife was popular—and others downright extraordinary; a spoon sold in Cherokee, Iowa, portrayed the local hospital for the insane. In addition, many businesses gave away spoons as advertising.

In about 1915 the craze for spoons began to taper off and by 1920 it came to an end. Today's collectors—we call ourselves spooners—have a large variety to choose from. Prices are equally varied. Least expensive are giveaway advertising spoons—most were silver-plated rather than sterling. A coating, or wash, of gold adds to

Enameling makes these souvenir silver spoons from the turn of the century desirable. Four are American-made, honoring (from left) New Orleans, South Carolina, Spanish-American War hero Admiral George Dewey, and the Civil War battle between the Monitor and the Merrimac. The one at the right, probably French, is a love spoon, a traditional gift from a suitor. Admiral Dewey appears on many souvenir spoons, but the one shown here is especially valued for its intricate decoration and because it was made from sterling silver by Gorham Mfg. Company.

a spoon's value, as does the mark of a famous maker.

But insofar as spooners are concerned, design generally outweighs the intrinsic value of the metal. A handle that is shaped into a design makes a spoon more valuable than one on which the design is engraved. Intricacy of decoration on both handle and bowl is prized. Enameled illustrations are highly valued. Certain motifs are especially popular, such as those that portray Indians or miners. Occasionally a date commemorating a personal event such as a birthday was engraved on a spoon, and such dates add to the value.

Much sought after are spoons issued in limited numbers for a special event. One is a serving spoon made by Gorham Mfg. Company and sold in 1892 at a benefit for the Actors' Fund of America. No more than 500 spoons, their handles decorated with the faces of actors and actresses, were sold. One brought $250 in 1979.

Although many of these souvenirs were manufactured by now-forgotten firms, a great number bear prestigious names—Tiffany & Co., for example, as well as Gorham. Nearly all marked their wares.

One of the most sought-after marks is the figure of a witch that appeared on much of the work produced in Salem, Massachusetts, by Daniel Low & Co. Low, a silversmith and jeweler, was one of many Americans who, touring Europe during the second half of the 19th Century, were intrigued by the souvenir spoons offered for sale in many big cities. Low brought home not only several spoons but the idea of making them himself. In 1890 he produced his first so-called Salem witch spoon (cover), which used a figure of a witch not only for a trademark but also for decoration on the handle. This sold well, not only locally but all over the country by mail order, and within a year he came out with a second version. Both are very popular among today's collectors, though the second is more valuable because its design is more intricate. An example sold for $95 in 1979.

The same type of spoon sometimes is offered for less through advertisements in collectors' periodicals, which offer good leads to most souvenir spoons. Other sources for good finds are antique shows and flea markets. The best source of all, probably, is to know somebody whose grandfather, many years ago, never came home from a business trip without a small silver present in his bag.

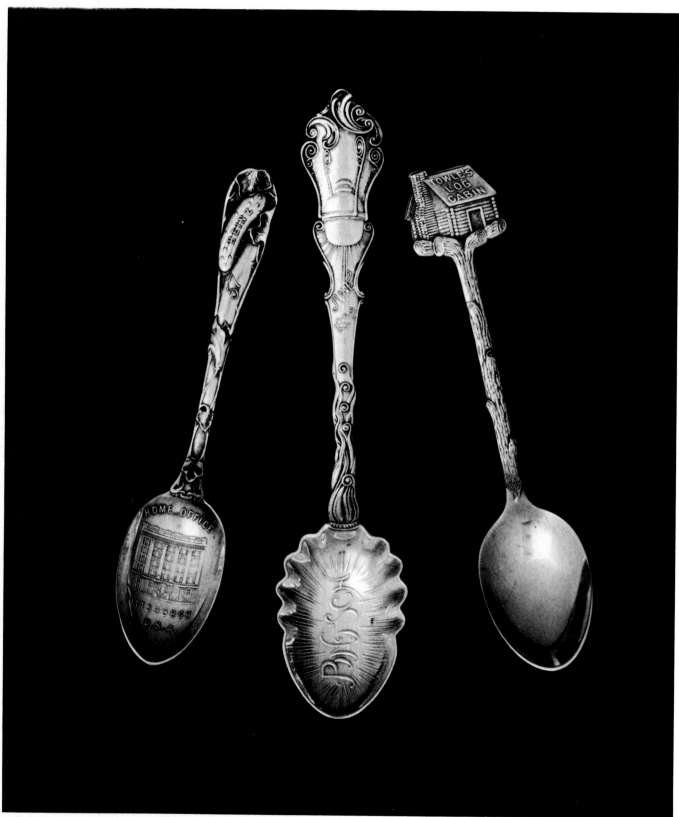

Silver-plated advertising spoons usually are easy to find. The H. J. Heinz Company's pickle-handle spoon (left) and The Towle Maple Syrup Co.'s spoon with the log-cabin trademark on the handle (right) are both common. The spoon in the center is more unusual—the gaslights invented by Julius Pintsch went out of general use before World War I. The date on the handle makes this spoon even more desirable.

Holidays are celebrated on three desirable silver spoons. The Christmas demitasse spoon (left) was introduced by Gorham in 1895 and kept in production; examples are impossible to date, though the dull patina on this one indicates age. The Easter egg spoon (center) bears on its back the witch's-figure trademark of Daniel Low & Co. The New Year's teaspoon was made by Alvin Manufacturing Company.

Apostle spoons, usually in sets of 13 (showing Christ and the Twelve Apostles), were traditionally given at baptisms. This Master spoon, depicting Christ, is dated, adding to its value.

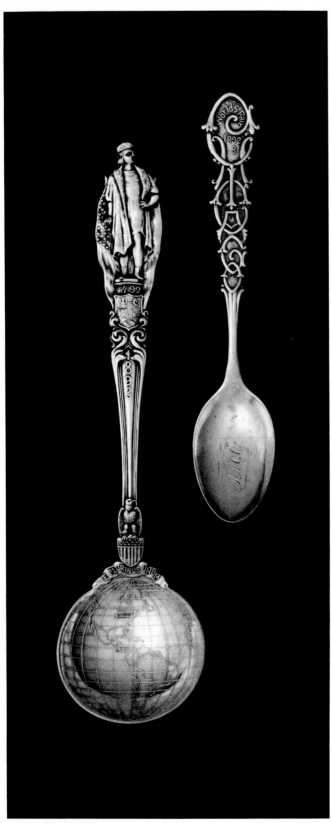

The most desirable of the many spoons from the 1893 World's Columbian Exposition is by Tiffany & Co. (left). The postponement of the fair from 1892 is indicated on the more common spoon at right.

Desirable historical spoons include Gorham's Gettysburg (left), with a segment of the Soldier's National Monument decorating the handle, and Freeman & Taylor's The Midnight Ride. Both were made in 1891.

Small spoons with portraits of George and Martha Washington were among the first American souvenir spoons. They were made in 1889 by M. W. Galt, Bro. & Company, which used the pictures as a trademark.

The portrait and signature of Mary Baker Eddy, the founder of the Christian Science Church, and the picture of her home make this spoon rare. Her credo, "Not matter but Mind satisfieth," is on the back.

Actor Edwin Booth appears on an 1894 silver spoon by Freeman & Taylor. The Hamlet quotation on the back—"I shall not look upon his like again"—adds to the value.

Norwegian explorer Fridtjof Nansen's expedition to the Arctic, requiring the three years from 1893 to 1896, was commemorated in 1897 by the intricate souvenir above.

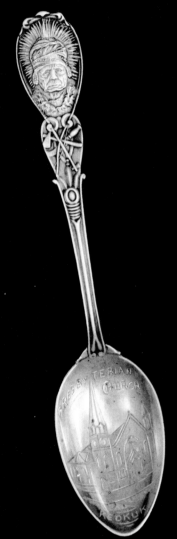

A handle shaped like the Statue of Liberty makes this New York City spoon desirable. Also valued is the detail in the coats of arms of the state (at the top of the handle) and New York City (on the bowl).

An Indian legend of a Seneca princess who was sacrificed over Niagara Falls is evoked in this scarce spoon. The sculpted handle adds to the souvenir's worth.

Indian Chief Keokuk, who sided with the Americans in the War of 1812, is shown on the handle of this unusual spoon. A church in the Iowa city named after him is on the bowl.

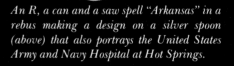

An R, a can and a saw spell "Arkansas" in a rebus making a design on a silver spoon (above) that also portrays the United States Army and Navy Hospital at Hot Springs.

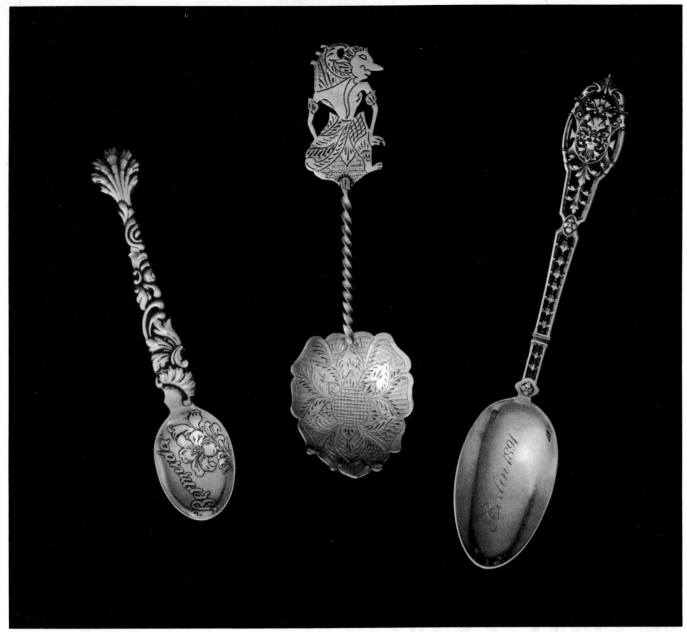

The undated souvenir of Bermuda (above, left) is prized because it was made by Geo. W. Shiebler & Co., a noted manufacturer. A Javanese spoon (center) is less valuable because it apparently is not solid silver. The date and gold-plating make the Berlin spoon rare.

MUSEUMS
The Passaic County Historical Society
Lambert Castle
Paterson, New Jersey 07503

COLLECTORS ORGANIZATIONS
Souvenir Spoon Collectors of America
P.O. Box 814
Temple City, California 91780

PERIODICALS
The Spooner, Route 1, Box 49, Shullsburg, Wisconsin 53586

BOOKS
Hardt, Anton:

Adventuring Further in Souvenir Spoons, with a First Glimpse of the Tiffany Souvenir Spoons. Greenwich Press, 1965.
New Discoveries in Historical Spoons: Souvenirs of the United States and Canada. Greenwich Press, 1978.
Souvenir Spoons of the 90's. Greenwich Press, 1962.
A Third Harvest of Souvenir Spoons. Greenwich Press, 1969.

Rainwater, Dorothy, and Donna Felger, *American Spoons, Souvenir and Historical.* Thomas Nelson Inc. and Everybodys Press, Inc., 1968.

Stutzenberger, Albert, *American Historical Spoons.* Charles E. Tuttle Co., 1971.

Staffordshire
China from One Corner of England

Elias Tobias, a Boston merchant, wrote in 1822 to a supplier in Staffordshire, England: "You have created a monster! My gates were stormed today by wives wanting dark blue Staffordshire china." A century and a half later Tobias' descendants, if they had carried on the business, might well find collectors storming the gates. The source of this highly desirable china is one small corner—a mere 12 square miles—of the English county that gave the china its name. There a supply of good clay and the availability nearby of coal deposits to fuel kilns combined to bring prosperity to hundreds of potters who produced a wide range of products from

---

Mrs. William Brink concentrates on the type of Staffordshire china called Historical Blue. She also collects spoons and ruby glass.

---

small ornamental figures to large soup tureens. (Traveling around in pursuit of clay, they dug up local roads, then filled the holes with shards of broken pots—giving rise, according to one account, to the word "pothole.")

From the late 18th Century onward, tens of thousands of barrels of Staffordshire china were unloaded on American wharves. So much has survived that many collecting specialties are possible. The most popular, by a wide margin, is the tableware known as Historical Blue, produced for export to the United States and decorated with American scenes. Some collectors concentrate on blue willowware, the familiar pottery decorated with an English interpretation of a Chinese landscape of a pagoda, a bridge spanning a river, plus willow trees, birds and a boat. Oriental scenes as well as other designs decorate another type of Staffordshire, called flow-blue, in which the image was deliberately blurred during firing. Other collectors look only for the work of one pottery such as Wedgwood (which is treated in a separate article in another volume of this encyclopedia).

Collectors who prefer a wider range of shapes and colors look for Staffordshire lusterware, iridescent pottery with a metallic surface often found as pitchers *(page*

The Nahant Hotel, a fashionable Boston Bay spa until it burned down in 1861, is bordered by spread-winged eagles and elaborate scrollwork in a Historical Blue plate made by the Joseph Stubbs pottery between 1820 and 1835. The illustration helps make this plate highly valued.

---

93); or multicolored pot lids; or the Gaudy Dutch tea or coffee sets made from around 1800 to 1850 for sale to the Pennsylvania Dutch. Other collectors choose chimney ornaments (figures for display on mantelpieces) or Toby jugs, named for—depending on which story you accept—Sir Toby Belch of Shakespeare's *Twelfth Night*, Uncle Toby of Laurence Sterne's *Tristram Shandy* or Toby Philpott of a popular song, "The Brown Jug."

Historical Blue began coming into the United States around 1820 and is found mainly near where it was originally imported, east of the Mississippi. The subject of the design, its sharpness and its rarity are important to collectors. The depth of blue counts heavily, partly because it is a clue to age, which increases value. The earlier blues are generally richer and denser than later hues. Many early pieces have surface bubbles, a slight dappling in the glaze and a bluish tinge in the white background. Around mid-century, technical advances in printing the design made it possible to mass-produce colors other than blue. Pinks, greens and browns arrived on the market, and the popularity of blue declined in America. However, today's collectors still favor the original blue, and most seek examples made before 1850.

Dating Historical Blue and the other forms of Staffordshire fortunately does not depend solely on subtle judgments of shades of blue. Some pieces bear the name or initials of the maker, or an identifiable trademark *(pages 90-91).* Since many of the firms went out of business or changed their marks after a few years, the mark is good evidence of the date of manufacture.

Even if the piece has no maker's identification, other marks may help date it. Most of these clues indicate a date before which the pottery could not have been made, separating the more recent from the very old. For example, marks based on the British royal coat of arms came into general use only in the 19th Century, and marks specifying a pattern name, about 1810. The Staffordshire knot mark and the word "royal" were seldom used until the middle of the 19th Century, "limited" or its abbreviations not until after 1860, "trademark" not until after about 1875, and registry numbers not until after 1884. Pottery was rarely identified as bone china or as of English manufacture until about 1900.

Such clear indications of when and by whom Stafford-

Part of the decoration on this plate—figures representing America and Independence, a miniature portrait of George Washington held by the figure on the left, and a looped border that shows the names of 15 states—was doubtless intended to enhance the appeal to Americans. The inset scene, however, is probably an English manor house.

Although these cup plates—used to hold emptied cups—are products of the noted Enoch Wood pottery and share the same view, the piece at left is more valuable. The blue is deeper and contrasts more with the light areas, the picture is sharper, and the shell border is Wood's best-known trademark. The scene depicts New York's Battery waterfront with historic Castle Garden, at the time a social center and theater.

shire was produced are listed in reference books *(page 97).* But the many unmarked or confusingly marked pieces still can be identified by their patterns or other aspects of appearance. Enoch Wood and Sons, a prominent exporter during the early 19th Century, framed his scenes with a shell design until about 1830; thereafter he frequently used a frame that was a pattern of flowers and vines. The brothers James and Ralph Clews, active from around 1818 to 1836, adorned their pieces with birds, roses and scrolls, and in some pieces included scenic medallions or scalloped borders decorated with the names of 15 states separated by stars.

Similar clues help identify willowware, which has been produced by the thousands of tons from the late 18th Century to the present day, not only in Staffordshire but in Japan, the United States and elsewhere. Josiah Spode, for example, used a simple perforated border until 1805; afterward a dragon and butterfly became the border pattern.

For dating Staffordshire figures such as Toby jugs and chimney ornaments, the technique of glazing can indicate age to a practiced eye. The earliest chimney ornaments and Toby jugs were made with colored glazes. Around 1790, a clear glaze over colors came into use, and after about 1840 cruder decoration, created by a technique that combined enamel painting under and over glaze, began to predominate.

A more intriguing method of identification can be applied to some Staffordshire figures. Many are portraits of noted or notorious personages. A surprising number commemorate scandalous crimes of 19th Century England and depict the criminal, his victim and the site of the deed, all labeled. One group of figures includes William Corder, Maria Marten, whom Corder murdered in 1828, and the judge who ordered Corder hanged.

For related material, see the article on Stoneware in this volume, and the articles on Bells, Cats, Chinese Export Porcelain, Dogs, Frogs, Majolica and Wedgwood in separate volumes of this encyclopedia.

This platter has a picture of the Church of St. Charles in Vienna, with the Polytechnic Institute on the right and the Danube in the foreground. It was made by Ralph Hall, a specialist in Historical Blue decorated with English and European scenes. Although foreign scenes are less popular than American views, examples as fine as this one are desirable.

A sailboat glides past an observation tower (center background) on an estate in the Connecticut River valley on this elaborately decorated coffeepot produced by the Enoch Wood pottery. The firm used the same scene on creamers and sugar bowls.

Staffordshire potters appealed directly to local American pride by depicting community landmarks such as the Philadelphia dam and waterworks. The pitcher at right was made by Henshall, Williams and Company.

Although deeper hues increase the value of most Historical Blue Staffordshire, the light shade of this teapot from the Ralph Stevenson pottery does not diminish its worth—this style never was made in the darker blue. The picture is of the statehouse in Hartford, Connecticut.

The small leaf dish at left is willowware, the imitation-Chinese design, and is probably the work of the esteemed Spode pottery, which began producing early versions in 1785. The first pieces were dark blue but after 1810, the approximate date of this dish, the color was lightened. Any early Spode piece is desirable.

These three pieces are flow-blue, bearing Oriental designs similar to willowware but deliberately blurred by the addition of chemicals during firing. Mulberry-colored wares as well as blue were done the same way. The Edward Challinor pottery made the cup and saucer; Mellor, Venables and Company the plate.

From 1846 on, the F. & R. Pratt firm made lids like these for containers. They bear scenic views such as London's Holborn Viaduct or pictures appropriate to the contents—the young shrimpers (bottom) once topped a jar of fish paste. Pratt lids are readily available.

IDENTIFYING AND DATING STAFFORDSHIRE WARES

Much Staffordshire is unmarked and difficult to identify. Some, however, bears a potter's name or initials. Other pieces are marked only with the Staffordshire knot (right) or with some version of the symbols listed below. The dates are approximate, indicating use through World War II; if no terminal date is given, the mark remained in use thereafter.

STANDARD STAFFORDSHIRE
KNOT MARK

The identifying marks, which are listed with simplified company names, are grouped by motif, in an arrangement adapted from the Encyclopaedia of British Pottery and Porcelain Marks by Geoffrey A. Godden. In some cases, successor companies used the same mark; in other cases, unrelated companies picked up an abandoned mark.

CRESTS AND CROWNS

 SAMUEL ALCOCK
1830-1859
G. L. ASHWORTH AND BROS.
1862-

 EDWARD ASBURY
1875-1925
JOHN DENTON BAXTER
1823-1827
HAMMERSLEY AND ASBURY
1872-1875

 BARRATT'S OF STAFFORDSHIRE
1943-
GATER, HALL
1914-1943

 BOURNE AND LEIGH
1912-1941

 SAMPSON BRIDGWOOD AND SON
1853-

 BROWN-WESTHEAD, MOORE
1895-1904

 CROWN STAFFORDSHIRE PORCELAIN
1906-

 DORIC CHINA
1926-1935

 GRIMWADES
1900-
J. PLANT
1893-1900

 HAMMERSLEY
1887-1912

 HICKS AND MEIGH
1806-1822

 HICKS, MEIGH AND JOHNSON
1822-1830

 HICKS, MEIGH AND JOHNSON
1822-1835

 A. G. HARLEY JONES
1907-1934

 NEALE
1776-1786, 1820

 ENOCH PLANT
1898-1905

 THOMAS POOLE
1880-1912

 JOHN RIDGWAY
1841-1855

 ROPER AND MEREDITH
1913-1924

 ROYAL ALBION CHINA
1930-

 SALT AND NIXON
1901-1921

 WILD BROS.
1904-1927

SHIPS AND ANCHORS

 WILLIAM ALSAGER ADDERLEY
1876-1905
ADDERLEYS
1906-1926
HULSE AND ADDERLEY
1869-1875

 ANCHOR PORCELAIN
1901-1915

 ANCHOR PORCELAIN
1915-1918

 BRITISH ANCHOR POTTERY
1884-1913

 BRITISH ANCHOR POTTERY
1913-1940

 W. T. COPELAND
1894-1910

 DAVENPORT
1820

 THOMAS FURNIVAL AND SONS
1878

 THOMAS MORRIS
1897-1901

 JOHN AND WILLIAM RIDGWAY
1814-1830
WILLIAM RIDGWAY
1830-

ANIMALS AND BIRDS

 J. FELLOWS ADDERLEY
1901-1905

 T. AND R. BOOTE
1890-1906

 CHRISTIE AND BEARDMORE
1902-1903
HULME AND CHRISTIE
1893-1902

 J. DIMMOCK
1878-1904

 CHARLES FORD
1900-1904

 A. B. JONES AND SONS
1920-

 THOMAS MORRIS
1892-1941

 THOMAS POOLE
1912-

 ROBINSON AND LEADBEATER
1905-1924

 ROWLEY AND NEWTON
1896-1901

 GEORGE WADE AND SON
1936-

HANDS

 BUCKLEY HEATH
1885-1890

 SIR JAMES DUKE AND NEPHEWS
1860-1863

HUMAN FIGURES

 BATES ELLIOTT
1870-1875
JAMES GILDEA
1885-1888
GILDEA AND WALKER
1881-1885
KEELING
1886-1936

 BISHOP AND STONIER
1891-1936
POWELL, BISHOP AND STONIER
1880-1891

GLOBES

 BARKERS AND KENT
1898-1941

 CARTWRIGHT AND EDWARDS
1880-
JOSEPH HOLDCROFT
1890-1939

 GEORGE CLEWS
1906-

 GREEN AND CLAY
1888-1891

GEOMETRIC SHAPES

 CHARLES MEIGH
1835-1849
CHARLES MEIGH AND SON
1851-1861
JOB MEIGH
1850-1851

 POWELL AND BISHOP
1876-1878

 JOSIAH SPODE
1790-1820

MISCELLANEOUS

 SAMUEL ALCOCK
1830-1859
BURGESS AND LEIGH
1862-

 WILLIAM BAILEY AND SONS
1912-1914

 BISHOP AND STONIER
1891-1936
POWELL AND BISHOP
1876-1878
POWELL, BISHOP AND STONIER
1878-1891

 LONGTON HALL WORKS
1749-1755

 LONGTON HALL WORKS
1749-1755

 LONGTON HALL WORKS
1749-1755

 MINTON
1800-1830

 MINTON
1820

 MINTON
1845-1850

 MINTON
1850-

 SHAW AND COPESTAKE
1925-1936

 JOSIAH SPODE
1790-1805

 RALPH WOOD
1770-1790

A cup and plate are in hand-painted Gaudy Dutch, a rare type of Staffordshire made specially for sale to the Pennsylvania Dutch. It is hard to find outside Pennsylvania.

Made around 1730, an uncommon milk jug (above) is decorated in a low relief of Tudor rose and filigree. The design was applied by sprigging, a process in which the relief was molded separately and attached to the body with slip, or liquid clay, before firing.

The molded pitcher above, adorned with bell-shaped flowers, dates from the mid-19th Century. The molding joins are visible on both sides of the pitcher; this fact and the recent date of the piece make it much less valuable than the carefully crafted pitcher at left.

The iridescent pitcher above is a rare example of lusterware, decorated by an intricate process. After the piece was fired, platinum and touches of red enamel were applied, and then the pitcher was refired. Such metallic finishes were very popular in Victorian times.

The fondness of the 18th Century English working class for gin is documented by the gin bottle on this Toby jug. It is sometimes confused with the Martha Gunn Toby—named for a famous beach attendant—but Martha Tobies bear the insignia of the Prince of Wales.

A late-18th Century Toby—a jug holding a jug—is a so-called Pratt-type, after William Pratt, who first used these colors for figures.

The Hearty Good Fellow on this Toby jug, pipe and tankard in his hands, was a common theme among Staffordshire potters. This example dates from about 1830.

A likeness of the poet John Milton is signed by Ralph Wood, son of a potter of the same name and a prolific maker of busts, single figures and groups. Anything made by either Wood is considered a collector's prize, especially if it is signed and stamped with a mold number. The colored glazes date it to the late 18th Century.

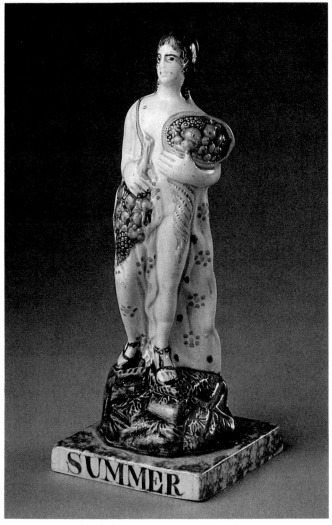

An allegorical statue is a valuable Pratt-type Staffordshire figure. Colored and then glazed, it resembles expensive porcelain.

Figures from Uncle Tom's Cabin were produced for the English market just before the Civil War. Though crude, they are sought after.

MUSEUMS

The Brooklyn Museum
Brooklyn, New York 11238

Everson Museum of Art
Syracuse, New York 13202

The New-York Historical Society
New York, New York 10024

Smithsonian Institution
Washington, D.C. 20560

BOOKS

Arman, David and Linda, *Historical Staffordshire: An Illustrated Check List.* Arman Enterprises, Inc., 1974.

Camehl, Ada Walker, *The Blue China Book.* Dover Publications, Inc., 1971.

Godden, Geoffrey A., *Encyclopedia of British Pottery and Porcelain Marks.* Crown Publishers, Inc., 1964.

Haggar, Reginald, and Wolf Mankowitz, *The Concise Encyclopedia of English Pottery and Porcelain.* Praeger Publishers, Inc., 1968.

Hughes, G. Bernard:
English and Scottish Earthenware, 1660-1860. Macmillan Publishing Co., Inc., 1961.
Victorian Pottery and Porcelain. Macmillan Publishing Co., Inc., 1959.

Larsen, Ellouise Baker, *American Historical Views on Staffordshire China.* Dover Publications, Inc., 1975.

Mountford, Arnold R., *The Illustrated Guide to Staffordshire Salt-Glazed Stoneware.* Praeger Publishers, Inc., 1971.

Oliver, Anthony, *The Victorian Staffordshire Figure: A Guide for Collectors.* St. Martin's Press, 1971.

Turner, H. A. B., *A Collector's Guide to Staffordshire Pottery Figures.* Emerson Books, Inc., 1971.

Stamps
A Collectible for Everyone

The numbers in stamp collecting are awesome. In the United States there are 20 million collectors; worldwide the total is perhaps 10 times that. Before 1840 there were virtually no stamps to collect; 250,000 designs had been printed by 1980—all of them collectible to some degree. Dealers in the United States number approximately 1,000, stamp-collecting clubs 35,000. Hundreds of stamp shows are held in the United States every year, and at one, Interphil—the International Philatelic Exhibition—attendance came close to 100,000.

As a result, stamp collecting is an exceptionally organized pursuit. Regularly issued catalogues *(box, page 123)* describe almost every stamp and list current prices. Long-established systems enable collectors to acquire stamps economically by mail. Most countries' postal departments have set up special agencies to fill collectors' orders. Commercial dealers send packets of stamps, each containing one kind of assortment, to collectors on

Consultants for this article were John W. Salomon, a New York stamp dealer and collector, and Ira Zweifach, who has served as president of The Collectors Club and editor of Scott's Monthly Stamp Journal.

approval; the collector sends back the stamps he does not want with payment for those he keeps.

The rarest stamps represent fortunes on tiny pieces of paper: The 1855 Swedish orange-yellow three-skilling stamp brought $500,000 in 1978, and it is not as valuable as the 1856 British Guiana one-penny black-on-magenta *(above)*, which sold for $280,000 in 1970. It is

Collecting by topic is a leading specialty of American stamp collectors; the stamps at left represent the 10 topics voted most popular in a poll of specialists. They are (from the top, left to right): space (USSR, 1961), scouting (Ryukyu Islands, 1965), flowers (East Germany, 1974), art (France, 1976), animals (United States, 1972), ships (Jersey, 1971), medicine (Republic of China, 1964), religion (Israel, 1969), birds (Mali, 1963) and Americana (United States, 1974).

Although it is disfigured by a heavy cancellation and clipped corners, the 1856 British Guiana one-penny black-on-magenta above is the greatest treasure in philately. There is only one of its kind known.

possible, however, to start a collection by spending a few dollars for a packet of 1,000 different stamps and to gradually assemble a collection without spending more than a few dollars for a single stamp.

Stamps of the type now universal were the brain child of Rowland Hill, a retired English schoolteacher who put out a pamphlet in 1837 to explain why the government's postal system was losing money. At that time postal charges were based on the number of sheets in a letter and the distance it traveled, and were usually collected from the recipient. Hill argued that postal clerks lost time figuring charges and that many charges never were paid because the system carried letters that recipients refused to accept.

Hill proposed a prepaid penny-per-half-ounce rate for all letters, regardless of distance. The postmaster general found this scheme "wild . . . visionary . . . extravagant." But it was adopted in 1839. Stamps and postage-paid envelopes were issued in 1840. Collectors appeared almost immediately, and 20 years later the first stamp catalogues came out; they showed that 1,200 stamps had already been issued by 100 countries, provinces and colonies. Their form has changed little since.

Stamps are printed by several methods, and each method creates its own kind of collectible variations. The variations can stem from the initial platemaking process or from the printing. To make up the printing plate, one image is reproduced many times, sometimes 400 or more, and slight variations can occur. In addition, some parts of the plate wear out faster than others and must be replaced or retouched, causing other variations. One stamp—the United States 1851 three-cent stamp—has 2,600 recognized varieties, and there are collectors who make these varieties a specialty.

Almost every stamp collection is specialized. The two most popular kinds of specialization are by country and by topic. Americans most often collect their country's stamps, but many Americans specialize in the stamps of a foreign country. Topical collections are built around

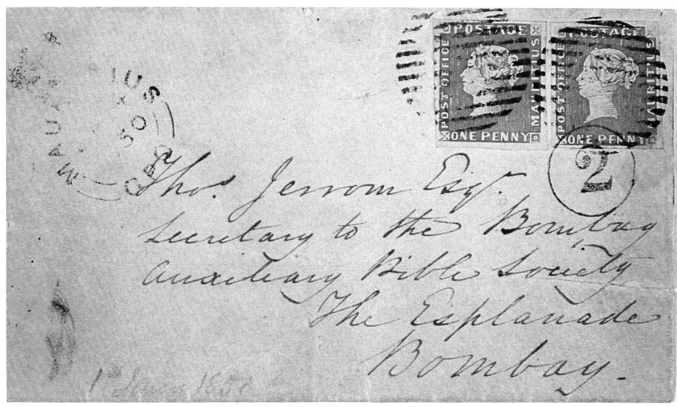

The most valuable cover —an envelope bearing its original stamps and postal markings —is the 1850 example above. The stamps are of the design that had been issued three years earlier by the British colony of

Mauritius, a small island in the Indian Ocean, at the insistence of the governor's wife. She wanted her party invitations to be up-to-date with the latest postal innovation.

one subject, regardless of country of origin. A famous topical collection based on musical subjects was that of Theodore E. Steinway, the piano manufacturer, who over three decades assembled a relatively small collection that was unique because many of the stamps bore the autographs of the people they honored.

Within each specialty, factors that influence value are generally the same. Stamps in the condition in which they were sold—these are called mint—are almost always more desirable than canceled stamps or even unused stamps that have been mounted. There are exceptions, however, for certain stamps are rarer if used. This situation can arise when a government demonetizes stamps—declares them invalid for postage before much of the printing has been put to use—and then sells them below face value to collectors. For example, the runaway inflation in Germany after World War I forced postal authorities to replace one issue after another with ever-higher denominations until the stamp for first-class mail bore a nominal value of 50 billion marks.

Telling a mint stamp from a used one is generally fairly simple—it has not been canceled, retains all its original adhesive and has not been stuck into an album with tabs called hinges. Other factors determining rarity, and thus value, require knowledge and experience. Some

stamps are rare because only a few were issued; others are rare because of some distinction introduced in printing deliberately or accidentally. Small differences detectable with proper tools *(page 102)* can make thousands of dollars of difference in value. Ordinary copies of the 1922 United States one-cent stamp, for example, are worth two dollars, but a variety of the same stamp, printed a year later with a slightly different perforation, was listed in 1980 catalogues at $6,000.

Stamps distinguished by errors are valuable because few mistakes elude quality-control inspections and find their way into circulation. One common error is the absence of perforation. Another is an inverted design element, almost always on a two-color stamp that has been printed from two plates, one for each color. If a sheet is sent the wrong way on one of its two runs through the press, the frame or the image in the center is printed upside down. The results are called inverted centers or inverted frames, but distinguishing between the two types is a matter of controversy. Some authorities claim they can tell from color or paper characteristics which of the two printings was done the wrong way. Others say the more prominent part of the design is generally considered to be right side up; if the center is prominent, the stamp is said to be an inverted frame, and vice versa.

In 1846, a year before the first United States stamp was issued, the postmaster of Millbury, Massachusetts, put out one of his own (above). Most such postmasters' provisionals, in use between 1845 and 1847, are rare.

The first stamps of the Hawaiian Islands were issued in 1851, when Hawaii was an independent kingdom. The two-cent blue above is the rarest. Intended to pay newspaper postage, it was also used for letters to the United States.

The Honduras 10-centavo was overprinted "aero correo"—an obsolete spelling of the Spanish for "airmail"—in 1925. Only one such stamp—collectors call it the Honduras Black—has been authenticated.

Among the most famous inverted centers is the 1918 United States 24-cent airmail stamp (right) called the Inverted Jenny after the World War I airplane, the Curtiss Jenny, depicted on it. A collector named William T. Robey bought a sheet of 100 at a Washington, D.C., post office on the first day of issue and immediately spotted the error. He pointed it out to the clerk who had sold him the sheet and then raced away to look for more. He found none. When postal authorities caught up with Robey, he refused to part with the stamps. A week later he sold the sheet to a Philadelphia dealer for $15,000. It changed hands again a week later for $20,000. In 1979 a single Inverted Jenny sold for $135,000.

Because errors like the Inverted Jenny are so valuable, forgeries are common. Perhaps the best-known stamp forger is Jean de Sperati, active from the early 1920s to the early 1950s. He took great pains. For example, he used bleach to remove the image from a common stamp and then printed the image of a rarity on the resulting blank so the paper would not arouse suspicion. When creating an inverted-center error, he erased the frame and reprinted it upside down—knowing that the greatest scrutiny would be directed at the stamp's center, not at the frame. Today de Sperati's forgeries are quite valuable collectibles in themselves, although not as valuable as the genuine rarities he was reproducing.

The greatest sale of authentic rarities was a series of 14 auctions, held over several years in the 1920s, of the collection of Count Philippe von Ferrari, a multimillionaire Parisian of Italian and Germanic ancestry who fled to Switzerland after World War I broke out. Dying there in 1917, he left his collection to the German postal museum in Berlin, but France confiscated the stamps as enemy-held property. They were so valuable that

An obvious printing error created the most valuable United States stamp—the 1918 airmail stamp known as the Inverted Jenny. A single sheet of 100 slipped past inspectors to become a collector's prize.

France agreed to deduct their value from the $33 billion of war-reparation debt assessed against Germany.

The auction of Count von Ferrari's stamps naturally interested collectors all over the world, including one who happened to be King of England. King George V badly needed one stamp from the collection: the 1856 British Guiana one-penny black-on-magenta. Acquiring that rarity would have crowned his collection of British Empire stamps. But an American outbid the royal collector. King George's collection remained incomplete, and the one-penny black-on-magenta went to America.

Tools of the Collector

Because stamp collecting has become so systematized, it requires some basic knowledge and a few items of simple equipment. An understanding of a number of technical terms *(opposite)* and of standards of condition *(below)* is necessary, as are certain books for reference and display as well as several devices that aid in the identification of individual stamps.

The tool that is indispensable to the stamp collector is one of the catalogues that standardize stamp collecting to an extent enjoyed by no other collectible. The reference most widely used in America is *Scott's Standard Postage Stamp Catalogue,* an annual four-volume publication. It lists and numbers nearly all postage stamps ever issued anywhere in the world (almost all of them illustrated), the current catalogue value of stamps both unused and used, and their dates of issue, perforation identification, color, errors and variations.

Among other important stamp catalogues is the *Minkus New World Wide Stamp Catalog.*

Two special tools can be used to help confirm the identity of a stamp. A perforation gauge establishes the number of perforations; one type has rows of dots against which stamps are matched. Watermarks *(right)* are made visible in a detector, a tray in which stamps are soaked in a chemical.

Once identified, stamps are organized in albums; a great variety is published to suit almost every kind of collection. Stamps can be mounted in the albums by attaching hinges, thin slips of lightly gummed paper, but because even the hinges cause some deterioration in the condition of stamps, many collectors prefer to slip their stamps inside plastic holders that are then fastened into albums. Stamps are never touched with the fingers, which might soil them, but are handled only with large tweezers called tongs.

RATING CONDITION

Stamp condition is classified into six grades, illustrated below. These factors determine condition: how well the design is centered; whether perforation teeth are bent, broken or whole; color; and how clear the impression is. On used stamps, placement and heaviness of the cancellation influence grade. An uncanceled stamp is graded higher if in mint condition—never mounted, with original gum intact.

SUPERB

EXTRA FINE

VERY FINE

FINE

AVERAGE

BELOW AVERAGE

WATERMARKS

USPS
USPS

Many stamps have been printed on paper bearing a watermark—a design that is integral to the paper, created by pressing a pattern into the semiliquid material during manufacture. The United States used watermarked paper between 1895 and 1916: the double-line letters at top (which stand for United States Postal Service) until 1910, after that the single-line letters. The regular issue of 1908-1921 can be found with either type and also with no watermark at all.

The presence of a watermark or part of one makes a difference to collectors; a Russian 1879 seven-kopeck stamp bearing a hexagonal watermark, for example, is very rare. Since the watermark is on a sheet containing many stamps, the individual stamps ordinarily have just part of the watermark showing.

THE TERMINOLOGY OF STAMPS

In order to understand catalogues, the essential stamp reference, collectors need at least a rudimentary acquaintance with such philatelic terms as those in this glossary.

BISECT: A stamp cut by a postmaster for use at half face value.

BLOCK: A group of at least four stamps, two across and two deep, that are still attached to each other.

CACHET: A decorative embellishment on an envelope.

CANCELLATION: A mark on a stamp showing it has been used.

CANCELED TO ORDER (C.T.O.): Stamps canceled as a service to collectors, without having passed through the mail.

CINDERELLA: Stamp not for postage, such as a Christmas seal.

COMMEMORATIVE: Stamp sold for a limited period of time, honoring a person, place or event.

CORNER BLOCK: A block from the corner of a sheet, the selvage (below) still attached. See also Margin Block.

COVER: An envelope with postal markings and stamps intact.

DEFINITIVES: The regular stamps of a country.

IMPERFORATE (IMPERF.): A stamp issued without perforation.

ISSUE: A stamp or group of stamps put out as a single series.

MARGIN BLOCK: A block of stamps from the edge of a sheet, the selvage still attached. See also Corner Block.

MINT: Condition of a stamp that has not been used or hinged and that has its original gum. See also Unused.

N.H.: Never hinged, i.e., never mounted.

O.G.: Original gum/adhesive.

OVERPRINT: Anything printed over the design of a stamp to change its validity, as, for example, to make an ordinary stamp valid for airmail.

PERFORATION NUMBER: The number of perforation holes for every two centimeters along the edge of a stamp.

PHANTOM: Stamp of nonexistent country—a fraud or joke.

POSTMASTER'S PROVISIONALS: Stamps created by a postmaster in lieu of government issues.

PRECANCEL: Stamp issued with cancellation already applied.

PROOF: An impression taken as a test from the plate.

REPRINT: A stamp printed from its original plates after it is no longer valid for postage.

SELVAGE: The border of a sheet of stamps. See also Corner Block.

SEMIPOSTAL: Stamp sold for more than postal value to earn money for charity.

SE-TENANT: Two attached stamps that are different. Some are the result of an error, but others are made intentionally for issues containing different designs.

SHEET: A group of unseparated stamps, usually 50 or more.

TIED ON: Said of a stamp on a cover canceled so that part of the mark is on the stamp, part on the envelope.

UNGUMMED: A stamp issued without gum, as opposed to a stamp that has lost its original adhesive.

UNUSED: Condition of a stamp that has not been used for postage but may have been hinged and may lack original gum. See also Mint.

The first United States postage stamps bore portraits of Benjamin Franklin and George Washington. Issued on July 1, 1847, they were not perforated and had to be separated with scissors. The firm of Rawdon, Wright, Hatch and Edson printed the stamps; its initials appear at the bottom.

Issues of the United States

The first postage stamps used in the United States were the result of an English businessman's enterprise. Henry Windsor, visiting New York City from London shortly after Britain's first postage stamps were issued, naturally found the American postal system backward—the mails were slow and there was no regular home delivery. He decided to stay and set up a private mail service for the city. On February 1, 1842, the City Despatch Post began its operations, offering prompt home delivery of letters for the price of a three-cent stamp of its own issue. Within a few months the service was carrying nearly twice as many New York letters as the Post Office Department.

The Post Office response was direct: It bought City Despatch Post lock, stamp and letter carriers. Operations were continued with the original stamps until they ran out, then with a design that was essentially the same but bore an amended legend, "United States City Despatch Post." By the 1980s an original City Despatch Post stamp was listed in catalogues at $750, a moderately valuable rarity among United States stamps. Others that have been equally significant in postal history can be found for just a few dollars, and every era can be represented in even a modest collection.

The most valuable among American stamps, bringing $10,000 to $100,000 when sold, are invert errors, special printings and also the locally issued stamps, called postmasters' provisionals, that were produced just before the appearance of the first regular issue in 1847. These precursors of the first United States stamps were issued under Post Office Department authority by 11 local postmasters from 1845 to 1847.

When the first national United States stamps, the five-cent Franklin and the 10-cent Washington *(above)*, appeared in 1847, postage rates were five cents for letters traveling less than 300 miles and 10 cents for letters going a greater distance. Anyone who finds an old letter in good condition bearing one of these stamps has found a collector's treasure.

The stamps of this initial issue were replaced by successive issues without fuss until the introduction of the 1869 series. It was the first of many that stirred collectors' ire. It deviated from the traditional type of illustration, a portrait, by including such other pictures as those of a locomotive, an eagle perched on a flag-draped United States shield, and a transatlantic steamer. Of the eagle-and-shield stamp, the *American Journal of Philately* said it was "the meanest looking stamp we have ever seen." The 1869 scenes were so unpopular that they were replaced by a new series of portraits a year later—and the 1869 stamps thus had the shortest life of any regular United States issue. Naturally they are rarer and more valuable than other regular issues of the 19th Century except for the earliest ones.

Five stamps included in the 1869 issue were also the first United States stamps to be printed in two colors, and therefore were the first printed upside down, with invert errors. These inverts—on the 15-cent, 24-cent and 30-cent stamps—are among the classic rarities of United States stamp collecting. In mint condition they can be worth more than 150 times as much as their correctly printed counterparts.

The year 1893 is a watershed for American stamp collectors: It was the first year in which commemorative postage stamps were issued and the last in which stamps were printed by private contractors. The first American commemorative issue was a set of 16 stamps that was released just before the beginning of the 1893 World's Columbian Exposition in Chicago. Postal officials and the commercial printer alike were denounced for producing useless denominations of two, three, four and five dollars—the highest possible United States postage at the time was only $1.28. The stamps have become quite valuable: The two-cent Columbian can bring a thousand times its face value.

In the midst of the uproar that arose over the Columbian commemoratives, the government's Bureau of Engraving and Printing was awarded the stamp-printing contract. From that time on, practically all United States stamps—regular issues as well as commemoratives—have been printed by the government, and for this reason many collectors use 1893 as a point at which to start or stop their collections.

The Post Office Department (which became the semi-autonomous United States Postal Service in 1970) began helping collectors in 1921; in that year it opened the Philatelic Agency, which announces new issues and provides first-day covers (page 114). This has not guaranteed completely untroubled relations with collectors, however. In 1934, for example, when America's most famous stamp collector—Franklin D. Roosevelt—was in the White House, his Postmaster General, James Farley, did him the favor of ordering special sheets of the national-parks series (page 111) for the President's collection. When collectors heard of this gesture, they objected strenuously. Farley calmed the storm by ordering that a special edition of similar sheets be printed for collectors. The original sets presented to F.D.R. and others, specially mounted and autographed by the Postmaster General, are valuable. But the ones that Farley ran off for the aroused collectors are not rare. They are fondly referred to as Farley's Follies.

The 1863 two-cent stamp is known as the Black Jack for its color and the stern face of President Andrew Jackson. Regarded as one of the most striking United States stamps, it is popular with collectors.

A mounted mail carrier—not a Pony Express rider—adorns this stamp from the 1869 regular issue, the first with designs other than portraits.

The six pairs of stamps shown above represent six consecutive regular issues. In the top row are Washington and Lincoln (1870-1873) and Jackson and Garfield (1888); in the center row are Grant and Sherman (1890-1893) and Washington and Madison (1894-1895); in the bottom row Jackson and Martha Washington (1902) and Franklin and

Washington (1908). (The next regular issue, from 1922, is shown in full at right.) Martha Washington's appearance on the 1902 issue was the first of a woman in a regular issue of United States stamps — although Queen Isabella of Spain, the patron of Christopher Columbus, had been depicted on an 1893 commemorative.

All 23 stamps from the 1922 issue are reproduced at right. They were the first regular issue after 1869 to bear pictures other than portraits. The high denominations are scarce and a full set is valuable.

Transoceanic airmail began in 1928 with dirigible flights of the Graf Zeppelin, and in 1930 the United States issued stamps for Zeppelin postage: 65 cents, $1.30, and $2.60 *(top). All are now valuable. Stamps for the first transpacific flights (center) in 1935, depicting a China Clipper, and for the first transatlantic plane service (bottom) are easy to find.*

The 10-cent special-delivery stamp of 1902 (above) depicts a cycling mailman. This stamp, issued 17 years after special-delivery service began, is especially valuable because it is in mint condition.

This parcel-post stamp is the first one to depict an airplane. Stamps specially designed for parcel post were issued only in 1912 and 1913; after that, regular stamps were used.

Confederate Postage

After the outbreak of the Civil War all United States stamps were replaced with new designs to prevent Southerners from using United States stamps that they might have in their possession. The Confederacy thereupon issued a series of 14 stamps for its own use, which created an unusual specialty for many modern stamp collectors. In design these stamps follow the American pattern, bearing portraits of native heroes.

Many of the Confederate stamps were printed in London and shipped to the South by blockade runners. Far more were printed than were used, so with a few exceptions they are easy to find and not very valuable. More highly valued are the Confederate covers that bear Southern postmasters' provisionals—stamps created by postmasters before they were able to obtain the regular issues.

Jefferson Davis, President of the Confederacy, appears on an unperforated 1862 issue. Other Confederate stamps honored Washington and Jefferson.

An 1893 two-cent stamp is one of 16 in the Columbian Exposition set, the first American commemoratives and the first to be such a large size. The high denominations are expensive rarities.

Many collectors consider this 1898 Trans-Mississippi Exposition commemorative the most beautiful American stamp. The image of cattle in a snowstorm is from J. A. MacWhirter's painting The Vanguard.

A 1907 five-cent stamp, one of three commemorating the 300th anniversary of the founding of Jamestown, Virginia, depicts the Indian heroine Pocahontas wearing European clothes as the wife of English tobacco grower John Rolfe. It is not rare.

A 1934 set of national-parks commemoratives depicts famous scenes from such tourist meccas as Yosemite, Grand Canyon and Yellowstone (top row) and the Great Smokies (bottom right). Even in mint condition, a complete set is fairly easy to acquire.

An expanding America is illustrated on three historical commemoratives. Above is the 1944 issue marking the 75th anniversary of the transcontinental railroad—the picture shows the flag blowing one way, smoke the other; at right are the 1953 issues for the centennials of the opening of Japan (top) and the Gadsden Purchase.

Prominent Americans honored on commemoratives include (far left, top) an early fighter for women's rights, a black scientist (far left, bottom), the famed maker of animated movies (left) and a noted composer.

Among military commemoratives are one of 1945 (top left) honoring the Navy for its role in World War II, and two noting anniversaries: the centennial of the Civil War (left) and the bicentennial of the Battle of Bunker Hill.

Space exploration has provided popular United States commemoratives. Among the subjects are the Project Mercury issue of 1962 (above), the 1969 moon landing and the Skylab orbiting laboratory launched in 1973.

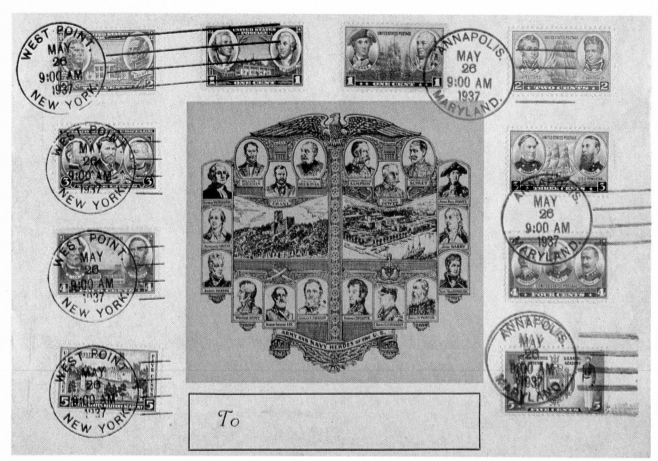

An elaborate cachet prepared for the Army and Navy commemorative series of 1936-1937 bears all 10 stamps in the issue. The two five-cent stamps in the bottom corners, the last of the series to appear, *carry first-day cancellations. This cover is unusual because it was canceled twice, once at West Point, New York, for the Army stamp and again at Annapolis, Maryland, for the Navy stamp.*

A Rush for First-Day Covers

Since the early 1920s the first day of issue of every stamp has been an occasion for philatelic celebration in the United States, and since 1937 the ceremonies have included the use of a special postmark: FIRST DAY OF ISSUE. Any envelope with a stamp canceled on the day it was first issued—whether or not it bears the special cancellation—is a first-day cover, often abbreviated F.D.C. F.D.C.s are one of the most popular specialties in stamp collecting, and they are particularly desirable if, like the envelopes pictured on these pages, they not only are first-day covers but also have first-day cachets—designs related to the event or person commemorated.

First-day celebrations are staged in places related to the illustration appearing on the stamp; in some cases they are held in several cities simultaneously. The stamp is put on sale in these first-day cities on the day of issue and is generally released at the country's 30,000 other post offices the next day. The first stamp that received FIRST DAY OF ISSUE cancellation was the 1937 three-cent commemorative that was issued in honor of the sesquicentennial of the Northwest Ordinance, the law that opened the Midwest to settlement. In Marietta, Ohio, 130,531 first-day covers were handled for collectors. The five-cent John F. Kennedy memorial stamp was specially canceled only in Boston, where 2,003,096 covers were stamped.

Postal workers will apply the cancellation FIRST DAY OF ISSUE on anything that has stamps on it, so long as it is what the Postal Service refers to as a hand-back—something that the customer brings into the post office to have canceled and then carries away. On at least one occasion the mark was obligingly applied to a collector's forehead bearing the appropriate stamp.

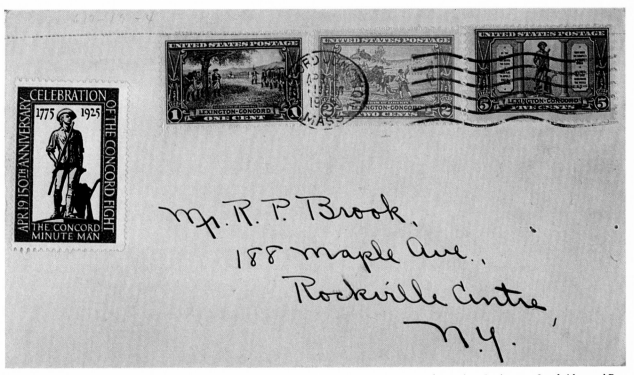

The three stamps of the Lexington-Concord issue, commemorating the 150th anniversary of those battles, were released simultaneous- *ly in Concord, Concord Junction, Lexington, Cambridge and Boston, Massachusetts. Covers from Concord Junction are the rarest.*

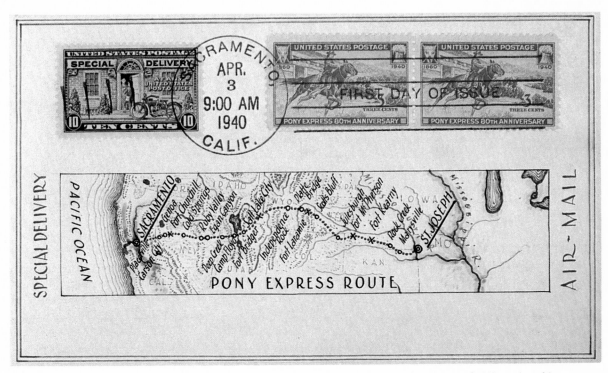

A first-day cachet for the 1940 Pony Express commemorative also bears postage for airmail special delivery. The stamp was *issued simultaneously at St. Joseph, Missouri, and Sacramento, California, the two terminals of the express riders' 10-day dash.*

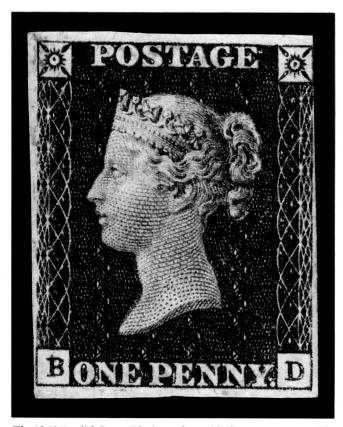

The 1840 English Penny Black was the world's first postage stamp. The Penny Blacks were printed in sheets of 240, each stamp bearing letters in its bottom corners to indicate its position on the printing plate.

Foreign Issues

American collectors who specialize in the stamps of one foreign country sometimes choose the country by happenstance. "I started collecting stamps at 10 years old," recalls one collector, "when an older cousin passed along his international stamp albums. I added stamps for a while and soon realized that I could never fill the thousands of pages. I looked through a list of specialized albums and decided to collect the stamps of Russia simply because the album for that country had the fewest pages. Of course, I didn't know Russian—I still don't—but I soon learned to recognize city names, personal identifications and denominations on the stamps."

Other specialists who concentrate on the stamps of a particular foreign country do so because of a family connection to the region or because of general interest in it. But many countries provide attractive areas of concentration for the simple reason that their stamps are un-usual or beautiful. Canadian stamps, for example, are noted for the beauty of their design. Great Britain and Brazil were pioneers in postal services and offer the oldest stamps. Some subjects—such as art in France or wildlife in Australia—are handled especially well by certain countries. And some nations cater to collectors, purposely making stamps that will be desirable to them.

Such countries as Tonga, the Cook Islands and Bhutan obtain much of their foreign exchange by issuing dozens of new stamps, often in unnecessary denominations, every year. They produce many more stamps than their postal services require, and they profit by selling the excess, unused, to collectors.

Collectors, in turn, profit from this deliberate overproduction of stamps by getting a variety that otherwise would not be available. The Tonganese stamps, for example, are exceptionally colorful and eye-catching. Tonga also leads the world in issuing oddly shaped stamps, everything from a banana-shaped stamp to a stamp in the form of a high jumper in mid-air.

But although such stamps are attractive, their value may be uncertain. Stamps from a country that prints primarily for sale to collectors rather than to fill its genuine postal needs are worth less to begin with, and probably will appreciate in value less, than the issues that are put out primarily for postage.

The methods of collecting foreign stamps are the same as those used for American issues. Stamps from almost any part of the world are relatively easy to acquire. They can be ordered directly from most governmental postal services around the globe. Dealers supply packets on the usual terms, sending groups of stamps on approval. And there are specialized catalogues—even specialized clubs—in the United States.

The potential for lucky finds may be even greater for those who seek out one country's issues than for collectors who pursue one of the other specialties. One rich discovery rewarded the collector who became fascinated by Russian stamps. "My luckiest moment came long after I had formed collecting relationships with many dealers. I kept these arrangements active by accepting envelopes of Russian stamps sent to me on approval for small sums, usually one dollar or less. Finally I accumulated such a pile of these envelopes, all unsorted, that I had to clear them out or be buried under them.

"Over several days I looked through all the stamps I had piled up. In a packet of various common stamps I found a 35-kopeck issue of 1902 that is usually worth less than a dollar—but this one had an inverted center. My hands shook—I was holding what turned out to be a rarity worth $17,500."

For related material, see the article on Lindbergh Memorabilia in a separate volume of this encyclopedia.

The first stamps to bear only a numeral as a design—bull's-eyes—were issued by Brazil in 1843 in denominations of 30, 60 (above) and 90 reis. Many collectors specialize in stamps of Brazil because it began issuing them so early.

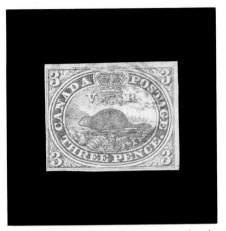

The 1851 Canadian three-penny red—the one above is from the 1852-1855 printing— was the first to feature an animal. Examples from this printing are less valuable than those of 1851, which are on slightly different paper.

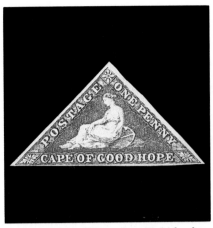

The Cape of Good Hope, then a British colony, issued the first triangular stamps in 1853. Although odd shapes were printed earlier in other countries, Cape triangles are scarce and are great favorites with collectors.

Cinderellas and Phantoms of the Stamp World

Stamps that are not good for postage—Christmas or Easter seals, for instance—are known to collectors as Cinderellas. One special kind of Cinderella consists of phantoms, which are truly make-believe. They are stamps purporting to be the official issues of countries that actually do not exist. Phantoms are referred to in philatelic literature as early as 1862; most of them are worth little or nothing, but a few examples are rare and accordingly valuable.

Some phantoms are obvious jokes, like the stamps of the imaginary Republic of Capacua, issued by a Belgian dealer named J. B. Moens in 1883. The date of issue, April 1, was carefully worked into the design. Other phantoms were produced with larcenous intent, such as the stamps of the Kingdom of Sedang (below, left), issued by a French soldier-turned-adventurer in Southeast Asia.

Several phantoms are long-standing mysteries. Among them are the one-eme stamps of St. Vanda, the few known copies of which are all postmarked "15/Jan/89." They have never been traced to anyone.

Stamps in seven imaginary denominations were issued in 1889 from Sedang, an Indo-Chinese country that was invented by a onetime French soldier.

Army Franks like this one look confusingly official. They were printed in 1898 by Major Brewster Kenyon as part of his campaign for special Army stamps.

Although Brunei is a real country on the island of Borneo, the 1880s stamp above is considered a phantom because Brunei did not start to issue its own stamps until 1907.

The stamps on these two pages would be essential for any comprehensive collection of France's stamps. The stamp at left, a design first issued in 1849, is only moderately rare. The 1900 60-centime stamp (center) is valued for its design, as is the 30-centime stamp of 1925 (right) —its illustration appeared on 15 denominations between 1906 and 1937.

French stamps are notable for patriotic themes such as those used for these stamps, which were issued following World War II.

Stamps reproducing great paintings, a series begun by France in 1961, make up one of the most popular continuing issues of any nation. These four were the first: The Messenger by Georges Braque (top left), Blue Nudes by Henri Matisse (top right), Cardplayers by Paul Cézanne (bottom left) and The 14th of July by Roger de La Fresnaye.

The three-candarin stamp above, issued by the Imperial Maritime Customs Post in 1878, was the first put out by a Chinese government. Chinese stamps are popular among collectors.

Still bearing the two-headed imperial eagle, this stamp was issued in 1917 by the short-lived democratic government that ruled Russia before the Communists seized power.

The 1928 Australian three-penny Melbourne Exhibition issue, a variation of a 1914 stamp, pictures a kookaburra, a kind of kingfisher. Australian wildlife stamps are desirable.

A 1930 Spanish stamp with The Naked Maja, Francisco de Goya's famous painting, was issued on the 100th anniversary of his death.

This 1936 Luxembourg 35-centime stamp is a semipostal—a stamp with a surcharge that goes to charity—here, aid for education.

The United Nations issues its own stamps. This one shows the stained-glass window made for the Secretariat building by Marc Chagall.

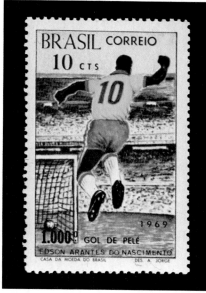

Brazil issued this 10-centavo stamp in honor of its famous athlete, Pelé, when he scored his 1,000th soccer goal.

Collectors prize Canadian stamps for beautiful designs like the one on this 1971 stamp, part of a set on the seasons.

ČESKOSLOVENSKO

Josef Lada 1887|1957
Divotvorný meč, 1926 - kolorovaná kresba
(B. Němcová - Národní pohádky)

1 Kčs

JAROSLAV ŠVÁB - 1970 - JAN MRÁČEK

A 1970 Czechoslovakian stamp pays homage to book illustrator Josef Lada with a design based on one of his illustrations for a folk tale, "The Remarkable Horse."

Among the hundreds of dance stamps from which a collection devoted to that subject might be drawn are those issued by (clockwise from top left): Turkey, Jamaica, French Polynesia, Czechoslovakia, Dahomey and (center) the People's Republic of China.

The 1956 East German 10-pfennig stamp (left) honored composer Robert Schumann, but the music shown was Franz Schubert's. The *mistake was discovered two days after issue, when a collector "played" the stamp. A corrected stamp (right) appeared 11 weeks later.*

MUSEUMS AND LIBRARIES
Cardinal Spellman Philatelic Museum
Weston, Massachusetts 02193

Smithsonian Institution
National Museum of History and Technology
Washington, D.C. 20560

The Wineburgh Philatelic Research Library
University of Texas
Richardson, Texas 75080

COLLECTORS ORGANIZATIONS
American Philatelic Society
Box 800
State College, Pennsylvania 16801

American Topical Association
3306 North 50th Street
Milwaukee, Wisconsin 53216

The Collectors Club
22 East 35th Street
New York, New York 10016

The Philatelic Foundation
270 Madison Avenue
New York, New York 10016

The Society of Philatelic Americans
Box 9041
Wilmington, Delaware 19809

PERIODICALS
Linn's Stamp News, Box 29, Sidney, Ohio 45365

Mekeel's Weekly Stamp News, Box 1660, Portland, Maine 04104

Minkus Stamp Journal, Minkus Publications, Inc., New York, New York 10001

Scott's Monthly Stamp Journal, Scott Publishing Co., New York, New York 10022

Stamp Collector Newspaper, Box 10, Albany, Oregon 97321

Stamps Magazine, H. L. Lindquist Publications, Inc., New York, New York 10014

BOOKS
Cabeen, Richard McP., *Standard Handbook of Stamp Collecting.* Thomas Y. Crowell, Publishers, 1979.

Collectors Institute, Ltd., *Pictorial Treasury of U.S. Stamps.* Collectors Institute, Ltd., 1974.

MacKay, James A., *Encyclopedia of World Stamps, 1945-1975.* McGraw-Hill Book Co., 1976.

Olcheski, Bill, *Beginning Stamp Collecting.* Henry Z. Walck, Inc., 1976.

Scheele, Carl H., *A Short History of the Mail Service.* Smithsonian Institution Press, 1970.

Scott Standard Postage Stamp Catalogue. 4 vols. Scott Publishing Co., 1979.

Steins
Reminders of Good Cheer

The steins opposite are something of a ceramic mystery. They were molded, but the designs look as though they were etched by hand, and the outsides appear to be three-dimensional but actually are smooth to the touch. These steins, a very desirable type known to collectors as chromoliths, were produced in the late 19th and early 20th Centuries by the Villeroy & Boch company of Mettlach, Germany, and hence are called Mettlachs. A similar mystery surrounds the company's cameos, or phanoliths, considered by many collectors to be the most beautiful steins of all *(page 127)*. They show portraits or small scenes in translucent white

Dr. Norman Medow, an ophthalmologist, has served as the president of Stein Collectors International.

clay set against either a green or a blue background. These not only seem three-dimensional. They are. But the portions that are in relief blend smoothly into the background without showing seams.

No one today is certain how these beautiful examples of the ceramist's art were made, although one authority believes the chromoliths were made from the outside in, by pressing clay against the inner surface of a mold. Villeroy & Boch zealously guarded its techniques; an account of the step-by-step procedure, known only to trusted employees, was kept in an Eighth Century building, a onetime abbey, where many of the steins were made. In 1921 a fire gutted the abbey and destroyed the documentation.

The company gave up production of chromoliths and cameos until 1976, when their popularity with collectors inspired an attempt to resume production of these specialties. But the secret was gone, perhaps forever. A limited run of reproductions of the old chromoliths turned out what are obviously just good imitations. (The 1976 reproductions are easily identified; the date is stamped on the bottom.)

There is no mystery surrounding the general techniques for producing other kinds of steins. They have been made from earthenware *(Steingut)* or stoneware *(Steinzeug)*—hence "stein"—ever since the 13th Century; later, porcelain, glass and pewter also were used. Examples produced during the 19th Century, the peri-

od that interests most collectors, have designs printed on the clay and protected with clear glaze. Steins made in this manner are known as pugs (printed under glaze). Another popular technique created a design in relief. In most of the very old examples, those made before the 19th Century, the raised parts of a design were fashioned separately and then joined to the vessel, or "looted," usually with the join marks showing clearly. More recently, the raised designs have been molded as an integral part of the stein.

All manufacturers used a variety of techniques. The chromoliths and cameos of Villeroy & Boch are the most prized. Those made in the late 19th and early 20th Centuries, before the 1921 fire, are readily identified by the trademark on the bottom, either an outline of a castle with the word "Mettlach" and the initials VB, or a head of the Roman god Mercury and the words "Villeroy & Boch." Collectors also seek the products of their competitors, including Merkelbach & Wick, Albert Jacob Thewalt and Simon Peter Gerz. All of these firms operated in western Germany.

Few steins were made in the United States; their rarity makes them valuable. Some collectors also look for beer mugs *(page 128)*, much more commonly made in America than steins. By definition a stein has a hinged lid, and its quality and condition affect value.

Steins from the 13th through 17th Centuries are extremely rare. Those from the early 1800s are somber in design and not widely sought. What collectors look for are the colorful items made from 1870 on, with depictions of rowdy drinking sessions, wedding parties, animals, buildings and people. In the early 1890s the manufacturers turned to occupational steins, the designs of which reflected the trade or profession of their owners. In about 1900 hobby steins depicted golf, mountaineering, ballooning and bicycling.

Particularly sought-after steins are the so-called regimental or reservist steins *(page 130)*. First produced at

Two Mettlach chromoliths, steins with a handmade look by Villeroy & Boch of Mettlach, Germany, are rich in beer-drinking lore. On the one at left is part of a drinking song; the lid depicts a dueling student. The other pictures the dwarf Perkeo, legendary guardian of the beer barrel at Heidelberg Castle; the thumb lift is the lion of Bavaria's coat of arms.

about the same time as occupationals, they were personalized souvenirs of a tour of active service with the armed forces. Especially valued are regimentals with cavalry or naval motifs.

German-made steins can be found all over America because quantities were brought home by soldiers after World War II; others were imported here in made-to-order designs ordered by American businesses, including many breweries, and by sports groups. In fact, an old bar that is going out of business or an old fraternity house can be a good place to find steins. They also turn up at flea markets and yard sales. I once answered my doorbell to find a stranger standing outside with two steins in her hands. She had been to a friend's tag sale, she said, and everything else had been sold; at dusk she was simply given the steins because no one had bought them. Having seen one of my advertisements, she wondered if I might be interested. I was. Both steins were Mettlach chromoliths.

For related material, see the articles on Staffordshire and Stoneware in this volume, and the articles on Art Pottery, Belleek Porcelain, Bennington Pottery, Majolica, Pewter and Shaving Mugs in separate volumes of this encyclopedia.

A relatively plain stein is valued for the date 1815 stamped on its lid. It is in the traditional cobalt-blue glaze on a gray background.

German-made glass steins are increasingly sought after, though less valuable than fine pottery examples. The hand-painted one at left is rare and can be dated by its design to between 1820 and 1840; the irregular base and the bubbles in the glass indicate that it was hand-blown. The other two are pressed glass and more recent. The stein at right, made around 1900, is valued for its rich color.

Different techniques created these raised designs. The one at left, on a Mettlach of the 19th Century, was made separately and joined to the vessel. The subtle coloring and the skill with which the design is blended into the background make this stein much more valuable than the 20th Century example from Wick-Werke (right), which has a molded design.

The three-dimensional image of late-night revelers on this Mettlach makes it more valuable than the steins above because it is a cameo—the design blends into the background with a smoothness not attained by applied or other molded-on reliefs. Mettlach cameos were made with dark green backgrounds as well as blue; these are equally desirable.

Souvenir Beer Mugs

Beer mugs can be distinguished from steins by their lack of lids. Because so many mugs have been made as souvenirs, emblazoned with college crests, city seals and brewery advertising *(left and below),* they are easily found.

From about 1890 until Prohibition began in 1920, many American breweries gave away mugs; since Prohibition was repealed, similar mugs have been sold. The pre-Prohibition ones are more desirable, particularly those advertising obscure breweries. The decoration on the mug, rather than the quality of its material, is generally the criterion of value; however, some turn-of-the-century mugs are especially desirable because they are of high quality, imported from the premier potter of steins, Villeroy & Boch.

Desert scenes, possibly intended to provoke thirst, decorate a set of stoneware made for the Leisy Brewing Company of Peoria, Illinois.

This stoneware mug is valued because it is a souvenir of a brewery, Becker Brewing and Malting Co. of Ogden, Utah, that was small and now is out of business.

Elves frolic over a barrel of beer decorating a common mug that was produced by the thousands before World War I for the noted Milwaukee brewery.

The Enterprise beer mug above is valuable, partly because it holds a quart—few of that size were made—but mainly because the label is sealed within the glass.

Among the few desirable steins produced in the United States is this silver-lidded example made in 1895 by the Weller Pottery Company of Zanesville, Ohio, noted for its art pottery.

The Mettlach chromolith above is the collector's prize. Its design, which includes a beer-drinking mounted knight and a stoneware lid shaped like a castle tower, is very rare. It probably was made in the late 1800s.

A late-19th Century stein of porcelain is desirable for the elaborately hand-painted, gold-framed scene from the Odyssey on the side and the three goddesses on the lid. It is a type called Royal Vienna, but the maker is unknown.

A helmeted soldier is the finial on the lid of a regimental stein commemorating the service of a man named Lamb. The decoration includes portraits of Kaiser Wilhelm (left) and Grand Duke Ernst Louis, scenes of soldiers smoking pipes and standing guard, the city of Worms and its cathedral. Among the inscriptions are the dates of Lamb's tour of duty (1906 to 1908) and the names of his comrades in the 118th Regiment.

Among many sports steins are bicycling and ballooning steins (right). The 1898 cycling example, from Germany, has a porcelain bottom depicting a then-common mishap (above); its initials (L.A.W.) and design identify the Legation of American Wheelmen, a cyclists' organization.

Two steins made in Germany for American brewers (above) differ in value. At left, one ordered in the early 1900s by New York brewer George Ehret and bearing his picture is a fine Mettlach. The other, crudely made, is marked "West Germany," dating it to after World War II.

This Mettlach chromolith, featuring an alligator handle and a view of the old city gate in St. Augustine, Florida, is a souvenir stein ordered from Villeroy & Boch by the municipal chamber of commerce.

Steins made in the shapes of people, animals, vegetables and buildings all are known as characters and are valued by collectors. House-shaped *steins are extremely rare; only three like this one, decorated to depict an elopement in progress, are known to exist.*

A dental student owned this porcelain skull in 1900. It is one of the more unusual—and macabre—character steins that appealed particularly to German medical students and are very desirable to collectors.

The Maid of Munich, an irreverent recasting of the monk that appears on the coat of arms of that city, is a common character stein. The bunch of giant radishes that she holds represents a favorite munch to accompany the country's favorite beverage.

COLLECTORS ORGANIZATIONS
Stein Collectors International
P.O. Box 463
Kingston, New Jersey 08528

PERIODICALS
Prosit, Stein Collectors International, Kingston, New Jersey 08528

BOOKS
Harrell, J. L., *Regimental Steins of the Bavarian and Imperial German Armies.* Old Soldier Press, 1979.

Manusov, Gene, *Encyclopedia of Character Steins.* Wallace-Homestead, 1976.

Mohr, R. H., *Mettlach Steins and Their Prices.* Published by the author, 1978.

Post, Anton, *Mettlacher Steinzeug, 1885-1905.* Hans J. Ammelounx, 700 Dundee Road, Palatine, Illinois 60067, 1975.

Stoneware
Prized Wares of Oldtime Potters

One of the most indomitable women in colonial America was Grace Parker of Charlestown, Massachusetts. In 1742, when aged 45 she was left a widow with 11 children, Mrs. Parker resolved to pursue her husband Isaac's ambition to start the first stoneware pottery in the Massachusetts Bay Colony. He had died just three weeks after getting a loan to start the business, and she picked up where he had left off. She went into partnership with an experienced potter, built a kiln, and using the clay that her husband had bought at Martha's Vineyard, began mak-

Mary Hooper collects all types of stoneware, from commercial bottles for soda pop to jugs that are prized examples of 19th Century folk art.

ing wares. The experiment was a disaster. The kiln collapsed and the wares were ruined.

Mrs. Parker tried again; the kiln survived but the pottery buckled. For her third attempt, she used a different wood for fuel but this, too, ended in failure. A year had passed. The borrowed money was gone, and Mrs. Parker had to sell some of her property. Nevertheless, she decided to give stoneware one more try. She imported a different clay from faraway New York, where stoneware already was in production, albeit amid great technical secrecy. This time the firing of the pottery succeeded.

The widow struggled for another two years, all the while selling off her dwindling estate. Two of her children died. Then the French and Indian War broke out, cutting her off from the clay she needed. Her pottery finally failed. Yet, unbowed, she retired gracefully. Her many disappointments, she said, were "no other than what have usually attended such as have enterprized things new & uncommon, how beneficial soever thay may in time have prov'd to the Publick, or gainfull to the after-undertakers."

Grace Parker proved right. Stoneware, which is ex-

These three pots are highly prized for their decoration. On the pot at near left, the tree was brushed on and the birds were applied by stamping. The zebras on the pot at far left were trickled on—slip-trailed—a technique that was combined with brushwork for the center example. The zebra pot is exceptionally valuable even though, like some other rare pieces, it has a fine crack and has been bound with wire.

Cobalt blue wiped into incised lines on the early-19th Century jug at left, above, created the decoration, including two doves of peace, that makes it more valuable than its plain contemporary.

Less than three inches high, this jug is a rare miniature. It is glazed with the clay mixture called Albany slip, through which the legend was incised before firing.

ceptionally strong and nonporous, did indeed become beneficial to the public. Handmade stoneware provided the jugs, jars, churns and other utilitarian vessels that were needed by a growing America. In factories it was made into sewer tiles. Stoneware vessels were made in many parts of the United States in several forms—egg-shaped at first, straight-sided later—that now are prized by collectors. Style, color and design of a piece are factors that collectors consider, as is age—hand-fashioned stoneware was made until about 1890, when it was replaced by machine-produced wares.

The works of certain skillful potters are particularly sought. Among the "after-undertakers" whose products are valued are James Morgan, who was active in the 18th Century in Cheesequake, New Jersey, near Newark, and the Remmey and Crolius families of New York City, both of which were still working early in the 19th Century. Family businesses also accounted for sought-after wares made later in the 19th Century. Collectible stoneware was produced by the Whites of Utica, New York, the Nortons of Bennington, Vermont, and the Hamiltons and Joneses, two families who worked together in Greensboro, Pennsylvania, north of Pittsburgh. Southern contemporaries whose products collectors value include Thomas M. Chandler and Collin B. Rhodes, both of the Edgefield District around the town of Edgefield in the western part of South Carolina. In many cases, potters stamped their wares with their names or with those of their commercial customers, such as breweries;

many of these identifying marks are listed in reference books *(box, page 147)*.

Although origin and age affect the worth of stoneware, the most important factors in value are distinctive characteristics of the pottery, such as shape, decoration and glaze. To create smooth, easily cleaned surfaces, many vessels were glazed with salt. Shoveled into the kilns, it vaporized and sealed the clay with a thin layer of impermeable sodium silicates. Other glazes also were used. In the North, Albany slip—a runny, dark clay—sealed the interior of wares, where salt vapor did not always reach. In the South, where salt was hard to come by, potters coated the unfired pottery with a glasslike mixture based on sand and an alkali such as wood ash or lime. When fired, the alkaline glaze gave a variety of colors, including green, tan and dark brown, that could be compounded to create a look called tobacco spit—the colors appeared to have dribbled down the side.

More significant to collectors than glaze is decoration. Lowest in value are simple abstract patterns, floral designs and naïvely rendered birds. Higher in value are depictions of animals, people and patriotic emblems such as flags and eagles. Particularly desirable are combinations of these subjects. Animals were sometimes rendered by unschooled artists who had never seen their subjects. Maned lions with the stripes of a tiger or spots of a leopard delight today's collectors, as do unidentifiable fish with marvelously expressive faces.

Most of these designs were applied in cobalt oxide, a

A jug with a man-in-the-moon decoration (left), a design also known as Punch, is unusual. The design on the other, more common jug may have been based on calligraphy exercises that were popular in the second half of the 19th Century, when both vessels were made. The lettering on the shoulder of the Punch jug is the pottery name; that on the other is probably the name of the merchant for whom it was made.

pigment able to withstand the high temperatures at which stoneware had to be fired, turning a beautiful deep blue. Occasionally, purple or green from manganese or copper was used as a second color; two-colored wares are very desirable.

The techniques employed in decorating stoneware changed through the years, again with a difference between North and South. The early Northern wares usually had their patterns incised or stamped into damp clay; then the lines alone or the lines plus the surface were colored with cobalt oxide. In later wares the pattern was brushed on or slip-trailed—the coloring was trickled onto the unfired clay from a cup that was fitted with a quill for a spout. After the 1850s stencils were used, particularly in southwestern Pennsylvania. Most early stoneware from the South is less decorated. Elaborate decoration sometimes is faked—a genuine but plain piece of pottery is given an overlay of design to increase its value, a deception prompted by rising prices for rare pieces. The fraud often can be detected because the added design will scratch off or even rub off under the pressure of a moistened finger; an authentic design, which lies beneath glaze, will not.

Stoneware collectibles are not hard to find at antique shops, fairs, flea markets or auctions. At any of these sources you might find so many choices that you decide to sit down and think about it. Have a look at what you are sitting on; in the 1870s the noted potter F. B. Norton produced imitation tree stumps as outdoor seats. According to the story, he personally modeled them, sitting down in damp clay in order to contour the design.

For related material, see the article on Steins in this volume, and the articles on Advertising Giveaways, Bennington Pottery, Bottles, Redware, Royal Souvenirs and Wedgwood in separate volumes of this encyclopedia.

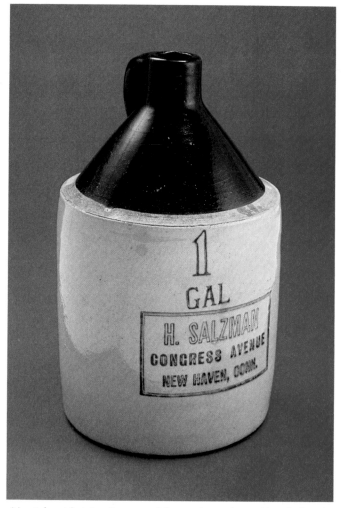

This jug, intended to hold batter, is desirable because it is decorated. The slip-trailed design suggests that it was made after 1850 in New York State, probably by White's Pottery of Utica.

A jug (above) bearing the name of the merchant who used it—"advertising," in collectors' language—is a type easy to find. The contrasting glazes are common on stoneware made at the turn of the century.

This late-19th Century jug glazed with Albany slip was probably used for syrup. Although it lacks the decoration looked for by collectors, its shape and graceful handle make it unusual.

A jug that resembles a tribal mask (above)—a grotesque—is rare and valuable. Although it is unmarked, the style is that of slave potters in pre-emancipation South Carolina.

The rippled finish on this jug, known as tobacco spit, was created by an alkaline glaze that appears to have trickled down the sides during firing. This kind of glazing is unique to stoneware made in the South.

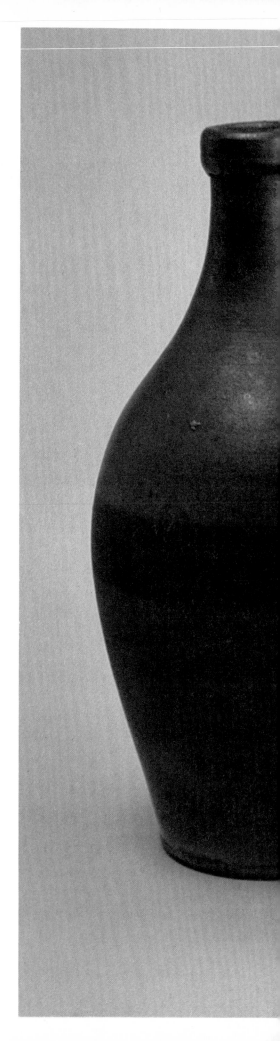

This rare flask bears the name of C. Crolius, a member of one of the earliest families of stoneware potters in the New World. All flasks are rare, and those made by the Crolius family even more so.

A progression in shapes of stoneware bottles through the 19th Century is illustrated at right. The egg shape was made sometime between 1800 and 1850, the 12-sided bottle after 1834, the California Pop bottle in the late 1800s and the ginger-beer bottle at the turn of the century.

W. Wallace Kirkpatrick's admiration for Thomas Nast's caricatures of the corrupt New York City boss William Tweed was expressed in this jug. Decorated with Kirkpatrick's famous snakes, the jug portrays or labels Nast (second from left), a bearded Tweed with some cronies, an anti-Tweed editor and anti-Tweed newspapers, some Tweed rackets, and a warning on the neck: "As in the past so in the future."

Imaginative Curios from Illinois

Unique among stoneware potters are the Kirkpatrick brothers, W. Wallace and Cornwall, who from 1859 until 1896 worked in Anna, a town in the southern part of Illinois. Although they made practical wares, the Kirkpatrick products that collectors look for are imaginative, even fantastic, novelty figures and miniatures. Much prized are one-inch-high log cabins and jugs, both of which came complete with decorations on the inside—a nude and the Lord's Prayer among them—that buyers could ponder through a lens built into each piece.

Most numerous of the Kirkpatrick novelties were pigs *(below)*. The brothers made thousands, most to serve as bottles and many decorated with railroad routes of the Midwest. The pigs were more than commercial products: To the brothers, one of whom was a staunch prohibitionist, the animals represented the evils of drink. The Jonesboro, Indiana, weekly *Gazette* summed up the Kirkpatricks' stoneware metaphor in an article about them in 1869: "It is rather a hoggish propensity to be guzling whiskey, and if the habit is indulged in, will soon reduce a man below the level of the hog, and cause him to wallow in the gutter." The evils of liquor—and in at least one instance, of political corruption *(opposite)*—were also portrayed in prized snake designs by W. Wallace Kirkpatrick, who collected snakes and put on snake shows.

A Kirkpatrick pig that doubles as a bank and a Midwest railroad map is very desirable. Pig and railroad-route combinations in the shape of bottles are far easier to find; thousands were made and many were given away by railroad companies in the Central states.

A water cooler (above) with an incised patriotic design is extremely rare, particularly so because of the extra details of a lion and rooster and the snake, rather than the traditional banner, in the eagle's beak. The cooler bears the name of J. Boynton and was probably made at his Albany, New York, pottery after 1815.

The cobalt-blue lion decorating this 19th Century butter churn, 18 ⅝ inches high, makes it very desirable to collectors.

A pot decorated in two colors (left) is rare. The absence of interior glaze and the style suggest that it was made in New York City at the turn of the 19th Century.

Stencils were used to apply decoration to stoneware in the late 19th Century, especially in Pennsylvania and the Midwest. This relatively simple stenciled piece is a fairly common type.

An otherwise ordinary jar (left) of the late 19th Century is given extra value by the thirsty bowler-hatted character shown on it. The jar is marked with the name of a pottery in Greenwich Village in New York City.

The molded bean pot above was mass-produced in Utica, New York, toward the end of the 19th Century and is a type easy to find. The designs near the rim were put on by hand with a coggle wheel.

A molded whistle (above), decorated in the desirable colors blue and purple, is a valued novelty. Bird whistles were made in Germany as well as Pennsylvania and upstate New York.

At the end of their workday, potters in factories producing stoneware sewer tiles used leftover clay to make unusual objects —whimsies— such as this head with a removable cap.

A baseball (below), also made from leftover sewer-tile clay, is desirable as an example of Americana. Other prized end-of-day forms include pigs, frogs, dogs and lions.

MUSEUMS
Bennington Museum
Bennington, Vermont 05201

Greenfield Village and
Henry Ford Museum
Dearborn, Michigan 48121

The Historical Society of York County
York, Pennsylvania 17403

The New-York Historical Society
New York, New York 10024

Old Salem, Inc.
Winston-Salem, North Carolina 27108

Smithsonian Institution
National Museum of History and Technology
Washington, D.C. 20560

PERIODICALS
Pottery Collectors Newsletter, P.O. Box 446, Asheville, North Carolina 28802

BOOKS
Barber, Edwin AtLee, *The Pottery and Porcelain of the United States and Marks of American Potters.* J & J Publishing, 1976.

Ketchum, William C., Jr., *Early Potters and Potteries of New York State.* Funk & Wagnalls, 1970.

Lasansky, Jeannette, *Made of Mud.* Oral Traditions Projects, Court House, Lewisburg, Pennsylvania 17837, 1977.

Osgood, Cornelius, *The Jug and Related Stoneware of Bennington.* Charles E. Tuttle Company, 1971.

Schaltenbrand, Phil, *Old Pots.* Everybodys Press, 1977.

Stradling, Diana and J. Garrison, *The Art of the Potter.* Main Street/Universe Books, 1977.

Watkins, Lura Woodside, *Early New England Potters and Their Wares.* Archon Books, 1968.

Webster, Donald Blake, *Decorated Stoneware Pottery of North America.* Charles E. Tuttle Company, 1971.

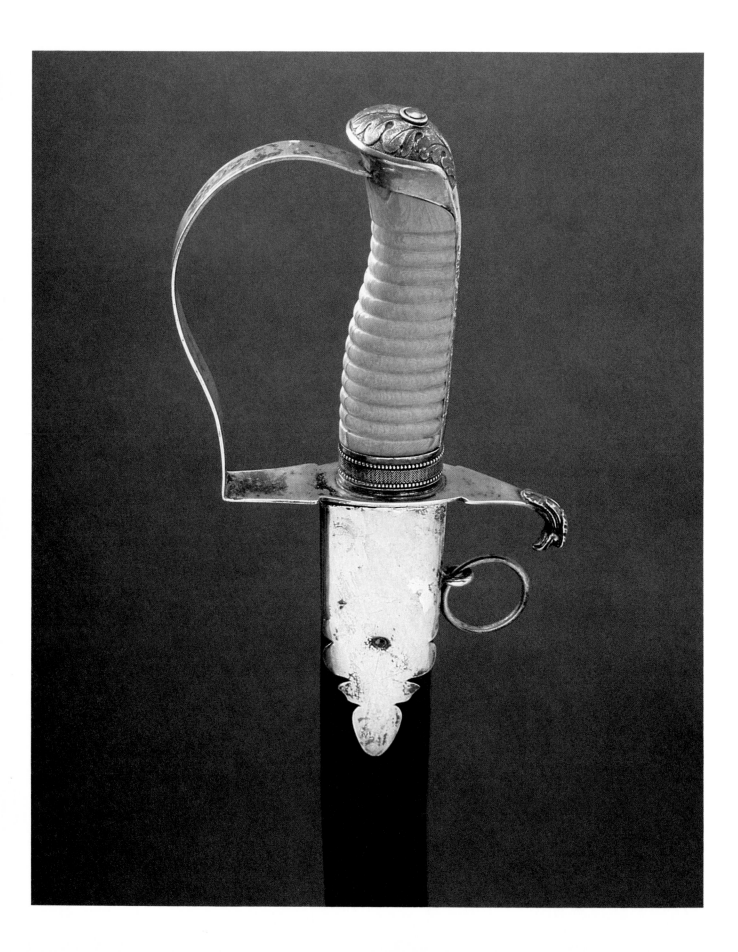

Swords
Traditional Weapons of Honor

Sir Richard Burton, the 19th Century British explorer, wrote, "To surrender the sword is submission; to break the sword is degradation. To kiss the sword," he added, "is the highest form of oath or homage." His words help explain the mystic appeal swords have for collectors. No other weapon is so intimately associated with honor even today, long after the sword has become obsolete as an implement of war.

Nowhere is this truer than in Japan, where the samurai, or hereditary warrior, treasured his sword above life itself, and such weapons are among the most desirable

---

David H. Bouldt, who began collecting in 1960, has acquired swords from every period since the Revolutionary War.

---

of all *(pages 156-157)*. American collectors, however, look mainly for swords of the American military.

The most valuable American arms are presentation swords, awards of honor not intended for combat; many of them have elaborately etched blades and hilts decorated with gilt and silver. Also prized are swords that officers had custom-made for themselves, in many cases beautifully crafted of costly materials. Other collectors specialize in swords made by a particular smith, such as Nathan P. Ames, who worked in the latter part of the 1800s; still others concentrate on weapons of one period—the Civil War is the most popular. Collectors generally group swords according to the wars in which they might have been used: the Revolution, the War of 1812, the Mexican War of 1846-1848 and the Civil War. Any sword from the Revolutionary period is very desirable.

Few of the weapons of that time were made in America; most were imported from Europe. Before the Revolution had run its course, however, swords were being produced by colonial cutlers, often working with imported blades. Accordingly, a blade that is marked Toledo (Spain), Klingenthal (France) or Solingen (Germany) but has a grip of cherry or maple wood wrapped in wire may be from the Revolutionary period. A few of

---

This officer's saber is especially prized for its silver hilt. The blade is believed to have been imported and fitted to the hilt in America around the beginning of the 19th Century—the eagle's head on one end of the cross guard, or quillon, is typically American.

---

these swordmakers signed their work, among them silversmiths John Bailey and Ephraim Brasher of New York City. The eagle, adopted as a national symbol in 1782, was a favorite choice of officers as an emblem on the pommel—the knob at the top of the hilt—and eagle-decorated swords are very desirable.

This period also saw the first sword that was produced under official United States government contract. In 1798, Nathan Starr of Middletown, Connecticut, was engaged to make cavalry sabers for enlisted men. He produced 2,000 of them, marking each "N Starr & Co" on one side of the blade and "US/1799" on the other. To find one would be a valued discovery.

A number of other companies also manufactured weapons for the infant United States Army in those post-Revolutionary years. Such contract swords, as they are known, are the specialty of some collectors. Contract swords, particularly the later ones, are not hard to find. What is extraordinary, however, is a discovery made by a collector in 1979. While examining a dealer's offerings, he found one that resembled a fairly common saber intended for dragoons, or mounted troops, and made under contract by Nathan P. Ames of Springfield, Massachusetts, in 1833. What made his find unusual, however, were the words "United States Dragoons Pattern" engraved on the blade. This sword had been made as the pattern from which all others of that model were copied. Somehow it had escaped into general usage.

By the time of the Mexican War, many other contract swords were made, including the desirable model 1832 foot-artillery sword *(page 154)*. Many swords from the early 1800s saw service again in the Civil War, and examples used in this conflict are not hard to find. Any swords made for the Confederacy are prized more than those of the Union because far fewer were made.

Clues to identifying a Confederate sword include the initials CS (Confederate States) or CSA (Confederate States of America) on the hilt or blade. Other identifying marks are the names of the Southern towns, such as Charleston, South Carolina, that produced weapons during the War years, and stampings or engravings of such symbols of the South as tobacco or cotton plants.

A maker's name on a Confederate sword, however, makes the weapon suspect. There are a number of fakes

The brass-hilted sword above is a prize partly because its blade bears the inscription "Grenadier of Virginia" (not visible), and partly because it probably was used in two wars. The sword dates from the Revolution, its leather scabbard from the Civil War.

around. In particular, a saber made by the Virginia Manufactorey from 1803 to 1820 and used by some Confederate soldiers has been forged many times. Both genuine and fake are marked "I Va REGt." However, the genuine sword has two fullers, or grooves, on the blade; most fakes have one. Caution should also be used when buying presentation swords; many plain swords have been decorated with fake inscriptions to make them resemble the more valuable presentation type. The authenticity of such swords can be hard to prove.

Discovering the history of a sword is one of the most interesting aspects of collecting and is not as difficult as it might seem. Many old American swords are engraved with the names of the owners; their official military records—some tell fascinating stories—are available to the public. Revolutionary records can be looked up if you apply in person to the Genealogical Library of the National Society of Daughters of the American Revolution; records pertaining to all periods before World War I are on microfilm at the Central Reference Division of the federal government's National Archives. Both sources are in Washington, D.C. The Archives will fill mail requests for information about a sword's owner if you provide his name, branch of service and home state.

For related material, see the articles on Civil War Equipment and Knives in separate volumes of this encyclopedia.

Although the blade at right bears the stars and moon used by Spanish cutlers, its cherry-wood grip wrapped in wire is American. The sword probably was put together in America for a Revolutionary War soldier.

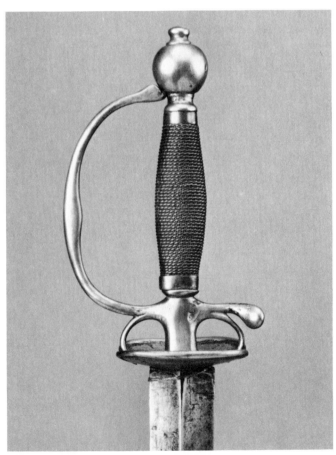

The style of hilt shown above is typical of smallswords that were worn by officers during the Revolutionary War. Made in Europe, it is similar to many that are fairly easy to find.

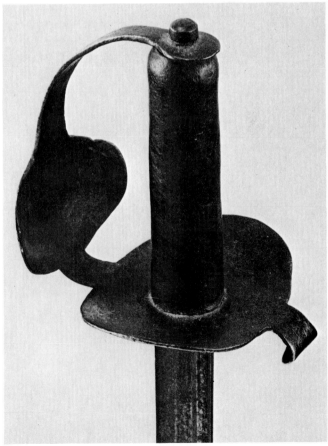

This iron naval cutlass from the Revolutionary War is unusual, but its crude workmanship diminishes its appeal for some collectors. It probably was made by a colonial blacksmith copying a British model.

THREE TYPES OF SWORD

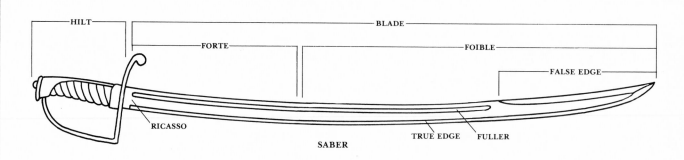

HILT | FORTE | BLADE | FOIBLE | FALSE EDGE

RICASSO | TRUE EDGE | FULLER

SABER

STRAIGHT-EDGED SWORD

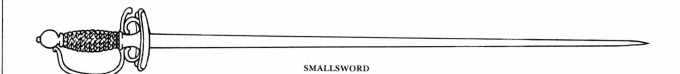

SMALLSWORD

SMALLSWORD BLADE SHAPES IN CROSS SECTION

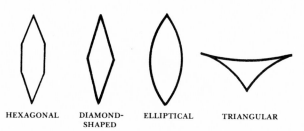

HEXAGONAL   DIAMOND-SHAPED   ELLIPTICAL   TRIANGULAR

The finial in the shape of a clock on the pommel of this officer's saber (far left) identifies it as the work of a Connecticut clockmaker who turned swordsmith during the Revolution. The Revolutionary-era scabbard, although incomplete, is also valuable.

THE ANCIENT STRUCTURE OF THE SWORD

The two essential parts of the sword are a hilt to hold it by and a blade, and have been since the first was made in the Bronze Age. Over the millennia since, many different designs have evolved, but those that most interest American collectors were incorporated in three military weapons of the 18th and 19th Centuries: the cavalry saber, straight-edged sword and smallsword (left), each intended for a different purpose. The saber has a curved blade suited to the cutting swing of a man on horseback; it has one sharp, "true," edge on the outer side of the curve. The straight-edged sword generally was issued to foot soldiers; it has sharp edges on both sides of the blade for cutting in either direction and a point for thrusting, like a spear. The small-sword, favored by officers, was a thrusting rather than a cutting weapon, and its blade might have any of several shapes (bottom left).

Identification of a sword may depend on construction details, some of which have such archaic names as pas-d'âne, langet and quillon, terms that describe parts of a guard (below). In more frequent use among collectors are words for features of the blade: forte and foible, for the upper and lower halves of a saber blade; fuller, for the groove in the saber blade; and ricasso, for the unsharpened upper end of any blade—a common location for marks indicating date of manufacture, model, maker and owner.

By the time of the Civil War, sword hilts and blades had reached the peak of their technological efficiency, and changed little thereafter. There was no longer any need for improvement, for by then the development of accurate, rapid-firing rifles and pistols had made swords obsolete as weapons of warfare.

PARTS OF THE HILT

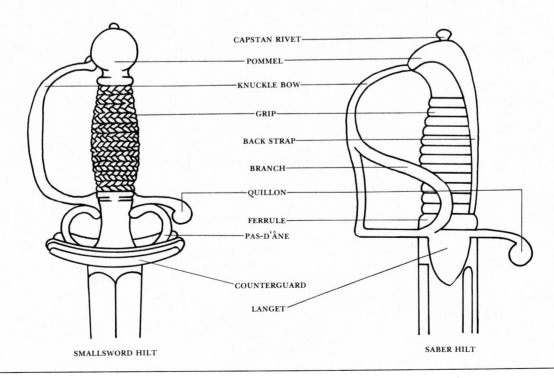

CAPSTAN RIVET

POMMEL

KNUCKLE BOW

GRIP

BACK STRAP

BRANCH

QUILLON

FERRULE

PAS-D'ÂNE

COUNTERGUARD

LANGET

SMALLSWORD HILT

SABER HILT

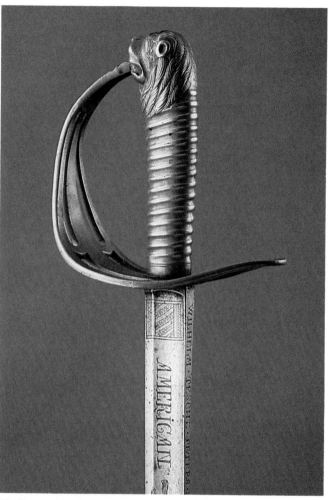

This nautically decorated, ivory-gripped naval officer's sword was imported in about 1810, probably from England. It is prized for its eagle's-head pommel and its rarity—the Navy had few officers then.

The lion, a British symbol, is an unusual design on the brass hilt of a post-Revolutionary sword. Made in Germany, it was trademarked "American Light Horse" to promote its sale to United States cavalrymen.

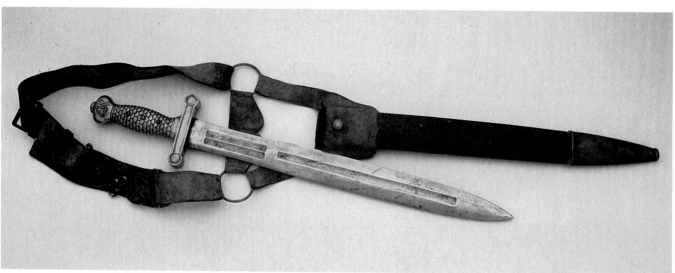

American foot artillerymen were issued this type of short-bladed sword from 1832 until 1870. Examples are fairly easy to find but are valued by collectors because of their similarity to swords used by Roman legionaries. The original scabbard adds to the value of the one above.

For Show Only

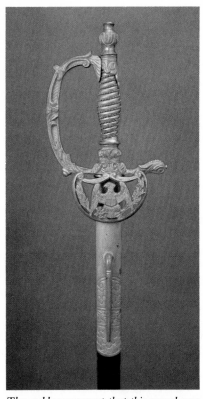

Among the most interesting of the special swords that attract collectors are those that had no connection with the military but were worn on ceremonial occasions by members of fraternal organizations or the diplomatic corps. Of the two types, lodge swords (as the former are known) are easier to find than diplomats' swords, which were never made in quantity.

From the late 19th to the early 20th Century, a great many lodge swords were made in America and Europe for members of organizations with an estimated total membership of more than seven million. Prominent among these groups were the Odd Fellows and the Freemasons. Their swords are fairly common.

The red cross on the grip above is a symbol of the Knights Templar, a Masonic group that wears ceremonial swords like this.

The emblems suggest that this sword was worn by an American diplomat. It was made in Germany in the late 1800s.

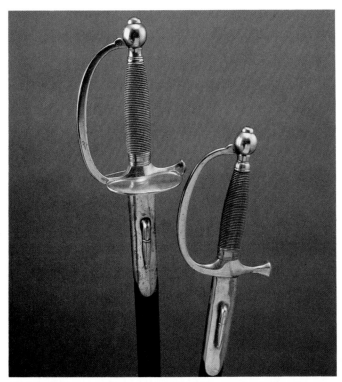

Slightly different versions of a model 1840 sword were issued to non-commissioned officers (left) and musicians until around 1900.

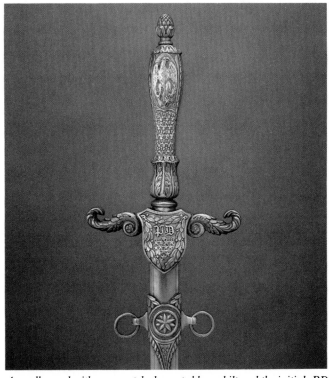

A small sword with an ornately decorated brass hilt and the initials PD was made for officers in the Army Pay Department in 1840. It is rare.

Once owned by a daimyo, or feudal baron, a ceremonial tachi sword is pictured inside its scabbard, which is set with cherry-blossom designs and lacquered w̶

Beautiful, Deadly Weapons of the Samurai

Among the most prized of all swords are those made for samurai warriors of Japan from the 12th Century to the late 19th Century. Despite their value, many are believed to be in the hands of individual Americans, who may not realize their worth because they were brought home as wartime souvenirs. After the surrender of Japan in 1945, all Japanese weapons were ordered confiscated. Later, "household treasures" were excluded, but by then the damage had been done. In the confusion, many valuable samurai swords disappeared—destroyed by Occupation authorities, lost or "liberated" by American GIs.

There are two main types of samurai sword. Fighting swords came in pairs called *daisho*, each consisting of a long *katana* and a short *wakizashi*. Ceremonial swords also may be long, called *tachi*, or short, *tonto*. The difference between very valuable handmade and newer machine-made swords is easy to tell. The blades of newer swords are a uniformly smooth steel gray, while handmade ones shimmer with col-

or, particularly along the edge pattern, or *hamon;* this wavy line of misty, often rosy gray—like a clouded sunset—reveals the uniquely hardened steel crystals that enable the superb swords to slice through armor. Scabbards also provide indications of age: Newer ones are made of metal or leather, older ones of wood.

Blades, even if separated from the rest of the sword, are so beautiful and valuable that they are sought for themselves. Japanese weapons were made to be disassembled with ease, and it takes only seconds to remove the decorative pegs *(menuki)* that hold the blade, then slide off the guard *(tsuba).* Although hilts as such are not collected, *menuki* and *tsuba* are. Each was made of various metals, but the raven-black *shakudo* (a mixture of oxidized copper and gold) is prized most. The designs on *menuki* and *tsuba* varied over the years and were dictated largely by what was fashionable at the time. The final choice, however, was left to the sword's owner, whose status and honor were represented by the weapon he wore.

This long sword, signed by a noted smith, Kin Michi, and dated 1812, is prized. Fighting swords are collected in pairs; the short wakizashi accompanying this katana is not shown.

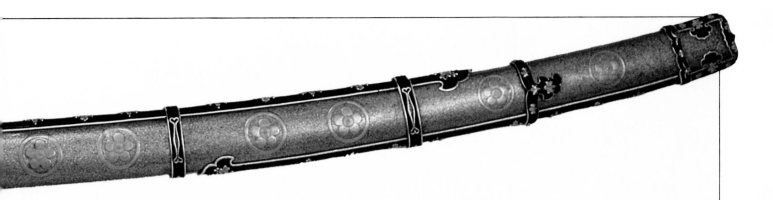

ld dust. The sword and scabbard were made about 1550; the ornate mount, through which the belt was threaded, was added more than a century thereafter.

Guards, called tsuba, from samurai swords are prized as separate collectibles. The one at left portrays a gilded dragon. The other is made in the sought-after black-copper-and-gold alloy and is decorated with a dragonfly—a popular design—a grasshopper and a ladybug.

Although variations of the model 1852 naval officer's sword are still used ceremonially, the one below, with a scabbard bearing the owner's name and the ships he served on, is prized.

The saber of a Civil War cavalryman is not difficult to find unless, like the one above, it bears the date 1859, a year when few swords of this type were produced.

A sword (above) presented to Civil War Colonel C. C. Marsh on his return home to Oswego, New York, is a unique prize. It was made by the well-known cutler Collins & Co. of South Canton, Connecticut, whose name appears on the blade. The blade's fine etchings and engravings picture a Union soldier with oak leaves and floral decorations.

A sword with a history is valued, particularly if it was used by a Confederate officer. This one bears the name of Midshipman J. H. Hamilton, who was captured three days before the end of the War.

Similar to the swords used by the Union Army, a Confederate weapon like this one—identifiable by the C and S (Confederate States) on the brass hilt—is harder to find because fewer were made.

Germany's imperial eagle can be seen on the guard of a saber (above) carried by a cavalry officer during World War I. The royal cipher on the grip is that of the King of Saxony. Such weapons, admired for their historical value, are not hard to find.

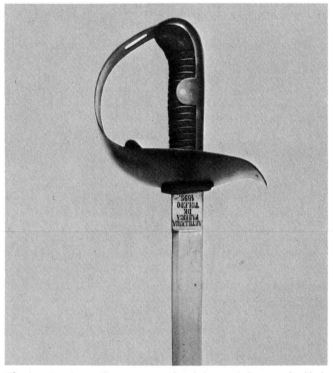

The imprinted "Artillery Factory of Toledo" and date on the blade beneath the hilt identify this Spanish cavalry officer's saber, a type used in the Spanish-American War. Similar ones are fairly common.

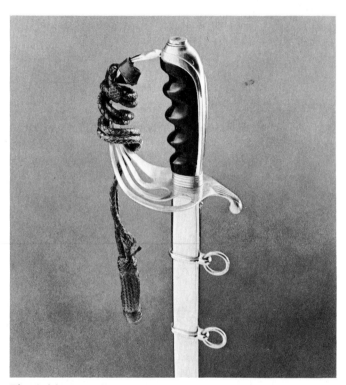

The model 1902 saber was a parade weapon for some American Army officers through World War II and is common. This example is desirable because it is one of few from the Springfield, Massachusetts, armory.

MUSEUMS
Fort Ticonderoga
Ticonderoga, New York 12883

The Metropolitan Museum of Art
New York, New York 10028

Smithsonian Institution
Washington, D.C. 20560

United States Naval Academy Museum
Annapolis, Maryland 21407

West Point Museum
West Point, New York 10996

COLLECTORS ORGANIZATIONS

Association of American Sword Collectors
P.O. Box 341
Delmar, Delaware 19940

BOOKS
Albaugh, William A., III, *Confederate Edged Weapons.* Harper Brothers, 1960.

Neumann, George C., *Swords & Blades of the American Revolution.* Promontory Press, 1973.

Peterson, Harold L., *The American Sword, 1775-1945.* Ray Riling Arms Books Co., 1965.

Wilkinson-Latham, Robert, *Swords and Other Edged Weapons.* Arco Publishing Co., 1978.